Behind the Walls
A Parent's Guide to Boarding School Culture

Tim Hillman

Second Edition

Copyright © 2004, 2013, 2014 Old School Press

ISBN-13: **978-0615758077**

Dedication

When I started to write <u>Second Home</u> more than fifteen years ago, my first call was to the late Craig Thorn, a Phillips Academy colleague who passed away far too young at forty-eight. Without his early guidance, a series of books detailing the culture of boarding school would never have been published.

The opportunity to create Second Home came from Louis Crosier, Avocus Publishing, and a dear avuncular gentleman, the late Ernest Peter. His willingness to take a chance on my nascent writing skills insured the publication of many books.

With great humility, I dedicate this edition of Behind the Walls to them, and to my sisters, Jane Bessette and Jennifer Potter. They lost a brother to boarding school and worked to understand the man I became living in a different culture.

A NOTE FROM THE AUTHOR

Creating a second edition of a book is a challenging proposition. As a writer and editor, you ask yourself- what could I have done better? How could I have explained better? Could I have moved the reader more? Is there enough commonality to evoke new and different reactions.

In the First Edition, I used rather hackneyed chapter names. I hated them early and often but was too lazy to make a switch. I discovered however that the vast number of readers were reading in one sitting. One hundred and some pages go down easily.

So, just few days before publication then, I ditched specific chapters in an effort to keep the reader in the same manner. They've been replaced with guiding questions that will keep you in a focused mindset throughout.

I also added material from three friends who experienced different kinds of boarding schools. Fearn Cutler deVicq attended the Southborough School, an early seventies attempt at a progressive boarding education. Samuel Potter attended St. George's School in the late 1970's.
George Spelvin is well known in the theater world.

Please remember that while their experiences are illustrative, they are not the only experiences students take from boarding schools. In point of fact, countless students commence from boarding school with purpose in their lives and the dedication that only a boarding school education can provide.

Preface

Christopher Tompkins
Head of School
The Perkiomen School

Independent schools have existed in the United States since colonial times. In some cases, our earliest schools pre-exist the British Empire, such as Collegiate in New York City, which was founded under Dutch rule. The American boarding school, a cousin to its British counterpart, is a bit younger, but its influence on the political and business leadership of the country remains significant – and well out of proportion to the percent of boarding schools within the independent school market and certainly out of proportion to the number of students in boarding schools within the total student population of the United States.

What is it about these schools that creates such an influence? Some would argue that boarding schools are the last bastion of elitism in America. Others would say that they breed leaders by virtue of the level of self-reliance and independence they instill. Still others would see these schools as mysterious links to our imperial past with strong vestiges of the White Anglo-Saxon Protestant tradition. Behind the Walls pulls back the veil on these mysterious beasts, of which there are only 200 or so left in the United States. Those that remain, though, offer unique educations, with each school having its own traditions, culture, and mission.

Like any school in the United States, these schools are filled with teenagers. Unlike public schools that are subject to district boundaries and state mandates and unlike day schools, which are subject to the "drive time" phenomenon, boarding schools are subject only to their missions, admissions criteria, and programs when it comes to enrolling students. Contrary to popular belief, boarding schools have a long-standing tradition of diversity, which began well before the Civil Rights era. Religious tolerance, even in most faith-based independent boarding schools, has a firm foundation. Since the 1980s, a focus and commitment on access and affordability have made these schools socio-economically diverse as well. The push toward globalism is old news in boarding schools, which have a long record of welcoming students from various countries from around the world. Students today arrive on jetliners, but most schools have stories of those who crossed the Atlantic and Pacific on ships and then boarded trains to these rural outposts of education around the USA, but mostly in New England.

So why read Behind the Walls? With no single mission, no single culture, and no single program to offer students, parents and applicants must work hard to determine what school to attend. How does a family without the "legacy connection" discern a strong school from a weak one, a highly competitive school from a holistic school, an "artsy" school versus a "jock" school, or even a school that will support particular learning needs versus that which expects the student to "sink or swim." And how do parents and applicants discern the permissive school from the authoritative model? Or fgure out a school's discipline policy on drugs, alcohol, and harassment? Finally, rather than depending upon contrived rankings or the ratings overheard at cocktail parties, how does an applicant find the right "fit" that will lead to success and happiness as a student?

Behind the Walls takes families and students into schools for the good, the bad, and the ugly of growing up. Tim Hillman pushes families to ask important, probative questions and to seek clear answers on the various topics that must be answered in order to enroll at a school that is best for the child. Some of what you read may be disturbing; some of it may even imply that boarding schools have "problems." All of what you read will lead you to the conclusion that boarding schools constantly strive to improve themselves and their students and that they have a key place in the educational marketplace. Like our exceptional institutions of higher learning, boarding schools offer the finest education to those students who truly want to excel in preparation for a college of their choice. With their traditions, academic demands, independent missions, and honor codes, boarding schools are safe and secure places of camaraderie, a la Harry Potter, where students grow, mature, and prepare for the expectations of college and the demands of life.

****

Why should I send
my child to boarding school?

Through twenty-five years of work as a teacher, one question was always a little difficult for me to answer. Whenever a student (especially a boarding student) asked why I went to a boarding school, I could never come up with a decent answer until now. My parent sent me away to school at fifteen. Except for brief interludes, I never came home again.

Here is the answer I give when people really want an answer. Conveniently, this answer is the truth. In 1971 I was a student at a rural high school in Rhode Island, heading down the wrong path. I didn't know that I was traveling that path, but in hindsight the move came not a moment too soon. My father had recently listened to a calling and had become an Episcopal priest. We had left our home in East Greenwich to live on a 200-acre farm in North Scituate, five highway miles distant from my father's church. Three years earlier, I had prepared to enter the Lockwood Junior High in Warwick, and follow my education through that school, on to the then-new Toll Gate High School, and hopefully off to the college of my choice. While that turned out to be the path many of my old friends followed, there was no reason to expect that my future would be different. In the rural high school though, life was drastically different.

While I was accustomed to one manner of program, Scituate introduced me to a different life entirely. Reflecting the needs of the community, the school offered a college prep curriculum but also took great pride in its programs in industrial arts and agriculture. Through my life, I have seldom met people that worked harder to put food on the table than the farmers that I worked with at school.

Indeed, I can say with pride that I actually know how to candle an egg, core sample a tree, use a chain saw with power and safety, and coax a large-mouth bass to eat a poorly disguised piece of wood or plastic. In my days in boarding school, those skills were not in evidence in my classmates. Of course my students in Tennessee were different- more than a few young men could wield a chainsaw far better than I.

My parents knew that Scituate was not prepared to meet my needs as a child and student. My math skills were in dire need of aid and my language skills not valued. North Scituate was not a place that a young man with an extreme interest in the theater was destined to prosper. The principal of the high school urged my parents to move me to another school for my sake.

Private school was of course the only answer. Naturally, Scituate had no independent country day schools, and Providence was an impossible commute for my family. If you know Rhode Island, you know that that winter days in the Northwest corner of the state are legendary. Getting to Providence , distant from snowy Scituate, was no simple task in the winter.

The local pharmacist however, had a son who attended St. Mark's, an elite boarding school in Massachusetts. The world of these schools was unknown to my father, but my mother, who grew up on a different side of the Great Depression, knew the world of privileged boarding schools. Together, they brought me to my new school for a visit, and the Headmaster decided that this would be my new home, even with my somewhat miserable grades from my ninth grade year. Years later, my mother revealed to me that the head of school actually paid my bills. I was stunned. Thank you Ned Hall. My admission was certainly a charitable act, and one that I hope has made that school proud.

The short story is that I was a suburban kid in a bad rural school situation, and there was no hope for a solution in the immediate area. If my education was to continue, boarding school was the only answer. It was not however, a panacea. For as much as the school bestowed the gift of an extraordinary education, I also received a drastically different kind of education that makes me typical of a lot of boarding school kids. That's one particularly good reason to send child away to boarding school.

If you cannot reasonably find a local school that answers your child's needs, look for a boarding school. What else? Homes are no longer defined in a simple way. Single parents are much more common, divorce is seemingly a rite of passage for some, and world travel is central to the employment of many individuals whose livelihood is tied to the world economy. If you cannot be at home for your child, and cannot find a reasonable substitute, look for a good boarding school.

Parenting is a far more complex art today than forty years ago. In that day and age, there were far fewer questions to answer, and vastly different demands on the parent. Today's parent can be overwhelmed by the reality

8

of parenting a child, or two or three. In our culture, the temptations that seduce teenagers are abundant. Parents must understand what is there, how to talk with their child about it, and what to do when things are not working. I hope that the great majority of parents feel that they are able to answer the needs of their children on a personal level. If you feel that is impossible, and find yourself setting your child adrift on this stormy sea of adolescence without any kind of life raft, look for a good boarding school. The school you choose should be able to help your child navigate to dry ground.

Sometimes, no matter how hard you try, your child is going to be far more difficult than you could have imagined. For whatever reason, her friends do not promote healthy behaviors, your attempts to discipline her are ignored and you find yourself wondering how all this strife happened. If this is your life with your child, look for a really good boarding school. If you choose well, you might just be able to salvage the child and the relationship.

These are only four possible reasons, and truth be told, there as many reasons as children that attend boarding school. Each child is an individual, and each demands a different approach. In choosing a boarding school though, be fully aware that the reasons that cover an area far greater than your child's academic life. When you choose to send a child to boarding school, you choose to allow that school to carry your child through their adolescence- arguably the most difficult years of her life. Do not forget the weight of that choice.

Your child will, for nine months of the year, be out of your home. She will be away from your nurture, away from relatives, grandparents and childhood friends. She will not wake you at two in the morning asking for Nyquil. She will not ask you to take her to a friend's house, and she will not wear her clothes in that way that just drives you crazy. You will not know what trip her school has arranged for her or what the value structure of her roommate will be. You will not be able to look in her face to see if he is lying, and you will not get a phone call every night, even though you really want one. You will not know what the money you sent buys and you will not be there to share a quiet snowfall. You will miss a lot.

If you are wavering now, good. That is the point. Deciding to send a child away to boarding school is never easy and the gravity of the decision cannot be underestimated. If however, the circumstances of your life, and your child's life, still make boarding school the superior choice, then find a good boarding school.

Should I involve my child in the choice?

I was a privileged kid going to an all-girls school in New Jersey with so-so grades. My family had a history with boarding schools, (father equals Kent, uncle equals Saint Mark's, brother equals Groton). In 1974 many of the old boy's boarding schools were just starting to go co-ed. My parents thought perhaps a "better" school would improve my grades, and I would make friends with some nicer kids. I think they felt I had a potential "bad attitude", and that a new environment would improve me, and relieve them of having to deal with a difficult teenager.

I was perfectly happy at Kent Place, but once I saw the Southborough School, I could hardly wait for Fall to begin. Over my 3 years, which were pretty happy, the boys school we were close to became a sort of home to me because of the drama program. I was very short, (I am still only 5'), and kind of immature, so drama was a great place for me to be myself, and encouraged to enjoy myself doing it. It had the added advantage of being something one could do over the weekend. New Jersey was too far to travel home for anything but the major Holidays, so I spent a lot of weekends "working on the play" to entertain myself. F.C.de Vicq

I grew from young boy to old boy in the guarded world of the American boarding school. At fifteen, my parents sent me from North Scituate Junior-Senior High School in Rhode Island to St. Mark's School, an elite New England boarding school. I attended as a full scholarship student whose decent (but not spectacular) grades made boarding school possible.

I stayed four years- starting as a homesick third form student and becoming, with the guidance of the adults, students, and children of St. Mark's, an accomplished sixth former on graduation. My classmates and I lived the life that was boy's boarding school in the early seventies. That meant getting up at 6:45 for breakfast, daily work crew, assembly, sit-down lunch, more classes, athletics, chapel, sit-down dinner, a brief break, study hours, another brief break, and then the sleep brought on by an endless day.

Little did I know then that boarding school would prove a major event in the definition of my future. After St. Mark's, I moved on to Bates College- a small residential, up and coming college that felt a little like St. Marks just bigger.

That was then.

True to form though, despite the changes in boarding schools over the years, the young people who attend them are strikingly similar to those I knew in my teaching days- possessed of the same adolescent insecurities as we are today (I'm still an adolescent). Some of your child's classmates will seem overly confident and hate themselves. (one particularly successful classmate of mine spent years working that one out.) Other kids are going to seem to recede into the woodwork.

Today's boarding schools are similar to certain schools in certain ways, and dissimilar in others. More than anything (and perhaps most expectantly) they mirror our own society. They are still most definitely boarding schools- institutions where you spend the formative years of your life shaped by adults and youthful figures that are, for the most part, unknown to you. For many of you, a boarding school will prove to be a major element in the definition of your future paths- whether you are parent or student, boarding school will affect you. A successful student at a boarding school gains riches far beyond those available in comparable day school situations. Boarding schools teach unique skills not taught in non-residential environments and students grow quickly in a fervent atmosphere.

At the same time however, ask yourself whether they could possibly achieve anything but that effect? When you place a large group of kids together in the same place for a lengthy period, the experience defines them, and that experience is powerful. Louis Crosier's excellent book <u>Casualties of Privilege</u> stands as a primer to the reasons that you should think hard about the reality of boarding school. In <u>Second Home,</u> a book I co-edited and wrote with the late Craig Thorn, and <u>Far and Wide</u>, also developed with Craig, students, alumni, and faculty members from independent boarding schools across the nation wrote about their experiences with boarding schools, both positive and negative. <u>Second Home</u> was a far cry from <u>Casualties of Privilege</u>.

Instead of exposing the dark side of boarding schools, <u>Second Home</u> worked to convey concrete ways that young people can and do prosper in the boarding school environment. <u>Second Home</u> found a niche and an audience. I am duly proud of the book, but wary of some many lessons it may impart. Ironic then is the fact that I am now writing this book- a book that proposes that you think long and hard before you send your child to boarding school.

Moreover, this book is also designed to be read by you, and even your prospective boarding school student. Boarding school should be an experience that you share- a partnership with concerned adults, positive, engaged students, and membership in a larger community that represents the school's many constituencies.

Do not miss my point- I cannot, and will not ever say that you should go to boarding school or send a child. That's not my call. The marketplace is filled with numerous boarding schools providing programs of education that are, simply stated, remarkable. Instructors are world class and often chose high school over college. However, there are many schools that should address major institutional problems before they prove worthy of your trust.

The Disisto School, a defunct institution in western Massachusetts, met with substantial public outcry owing to their methodology, including forced exclusion, physical abuse, and generally a lot of things that would make you say "What?" The outcry was not enough to close the school down.

Another, Overbrook Academy is run by a group affiliated with the discredited Legion of Christ movement of the Catholic church. Their educational mission continues- sometimes under surprising identities. You will not find that the school has any connection to the Legion of Christ. Simple question then- if the school will be less than honest in their dealings with the public, how will they treat their kids?

Be especially diligent if you are looking for a therapeutic environment, or are using boarding school as a means of dealing with problems at home. Frequently, problems at home and school stay problems at home and school unless the root cause is addressed. The worst part of that is that generally a school's ills are largely hidden from you by well-meaning individuals. They mask the bad boarding school and unfortunately, bad boarding schools exist. During the writing of this book, another boarding school in Rhode Island run by a religious order faces charges of mistreatment of its students.

Most difficult is the fact that discerning whether a boarding school is flawed is openly combated by every boarding school on the face of the planet. Take a good look at the view books and web sites. No matter what the school, they always-ALWAYS present the school in a light that attempts to make you believe that their school is the best school for your particular child. That's only natural, but it's propaganda at its finest. No school ever bears a completely true semblance to the school that they show you in the view book. You do not see the graffiti in the depths of a school's basement, the secret spots the kids hide from faculty, or the showers that date from 1935 and still run cold every time someone flushes a toilet. That is reality. Moreover, some of the things they miss tell a positive tale. That's a shame.

Boarding schools do not want you to know that reality up front. Instead, each private school is trying to sell you a product. You seldom see the actual product of such schools beyond graduates' laudable achievements. Such achievements don't happen only at boarding school. Sometimes, that truth is a remarkable success story. Each school can recite for you the stories of students whom they changed forever. Their school, they will tell you, is different. Parents will tell you the same thing. They are correct. They are not telling you, however, about the type of kid who is all too frequently ill served by a boarding school.

Boarding school faculties sometimes call these students "the ones that slipped through the cracks" predicating that belief on the idea that the floor of the school has only cracks, not gaping holes. For some this is true. Others? The cracks loom large and are, for the children, extremely attractive. More troubling is the fact that students at boarding schools effectively learn to live a double life. For the school, students present a certain picture. They behave, do their work- all the things the school expects.

Behind that veneer, you will often find a hazy secondary existence. Some people tell you that such behavior is normal, even outside of the boarding school, and they are correct. Each of us hides some manner of truth from the world. At a boarding school though, you will see that the temptations and risks can be far more troubling. Worst of all, you are at home, distant, and never see these changes within your child. Does one school stand out one way or another? Of course, but I am not writing to tell you what school to choose.

More accurately, I hope that my 40 years of experience with boarding schools will enable you and your child(ren) to develop a student-centric process of examining boarding schools with eyes unfettered by reputation.

If you fail to address school choice properly, you may make the worst mistake of all- placing your child at a school where he will not only get a less than superior education, but possibly an education that you never expected or desired. If you do not know how to interview the school, you may find yourself at the bad end of a good sales pitch.

Be aware also that sometimes the boarding school sales pitch is in direct opposition to the way boarding schools want you to view them. Throughout the independent school world, parents and students have come to view schools as sellers of a product and are likely to hold a school responsible for the education (and person) they pay substantial amounts of money to receive.

School staffs hate that state of mind. Although they will say the opposite, boarding school staff members do not always enjoy the input of parents, particularly if that input is negative. They will make the necessary calls and write the necessary letters, but one blessing for a boarding school teacher is the lack of contact with the parent body. Truth be told, many schools initiate contact with parents in order to cover their backside. If a child performs poorly, schools are held responsible by parents if the school has not informed them. No school wants to see parents at the complaint counter. If they do, they have assiduously prepared a methodology that makes the failure fall squarely on the student's shoulders.

Let us dig in then, and look at boarding schools, what they represent, what they are really like and what you can expect from them. I hope that you will make a decision that represents the most positive avenue for your child to travel, even if that avenue happens to be the local high school down the road.

What does a head of school do?

Hundreds of boarding schools in the United States offer a potential home for your child's educational future. Hundreds. How do you find the ones that are actually going to meet the billing? How are you going to possibly discern which schools are best for your child? Or even, the best for your child? A daunting question indeed.

Begin by looking at the leadership structure of an institution. In boarding schools, you do not generally find that the personal qualities of the head of school wholly define the school. However, the head of school is more than likely a reflection of the attitude of the institution. Remember, schools are run not by the head, but by the trustees who choose the head of school. To that individual, they entrust the good name, reputation and well-being of the institution. They do not take that choice lightly. Heads of schools often reflect the work of a large number of individuals, each of whom has a stake in the "right" candidate accepting the offer to lead the institution. The parties involved in the choice include professional consultants who screen candidates, faculty members and trustees who interview and examine credentials, and even parents and students in some cases. All of these individuals look for an individual who reflects either of two things. A school may wish to maintain the status quo of the institution, and therefore hire a head of school whose extensive background in education makes him or her a logical choice to keep the school functioning in the manner to which it has grown accustomed. When Ted Sizer left Andover in 1981, Donald McNemar came to the school from a substantial leadership position at Kenyon. Barbara Chase replaced McNemar in 1994 after a fourteen year tenure at Bryn Mawr Academy in Pittsburgh.

Possibly, they choose a candidate who already possesses an intimate knowledge of the school. Many a teacher graduated from a boarding school, had an illustrious leadership career at another school, a returned to lead his old school. He brings to the school a keen knowledge not just of educational practice, but also an alum's intimate knowledge of the school.

Schools may be rivals on the football or field hockey fields, but such friendly rivalry brings with it knowledge of the inner workings of another school. It is therefore far from unlikely to find that an Assistant Head of School at one becomes the head at another. Even in extremely large boarding schools, this familiarity can lead to hiring that maintains the status quo.

In schools that have not been extremely successful in recent years new heads of school tend to be younger and keyed in to the modern challenges facing boarding schools. This head of school is there because the institution demands change on a fundamental level- change that the former head was either reluctant or unable to effect. Where can you see the evidence of a reform head? Instead of looking at how many students the school has, or at the size of the endowment, take a good look at the number of faculty that stay at the school for protracted periods. When a reform head arrives, dead wood tends to depart. Quickly. A reform head makes fast allies and fast enemies on the staff. The only question is which group has the strongest will. A strong reform head will do just that- reform the school. A weak reform head will do just the opposite.

In those cases, a school in need of reform will dig in its heels and refuse to change. Students become allies of the faculty in such situations. Understand up front that these relationships are at the very heart of the school. Unwittingly, an alliance of students and faculty make it impossible for a head of school to effect any reform. The students openly rebel and at times, the faculty follows.

In at least one incident widely publicized in boarding circles, the faculty of prominent St. Paul's School rebelled against the then current head of school with a vote of "no-confidence" if the head's strong disciplinary actions continued. No doubt, you can predict the result of this action. The head resigned under pressure and the school went forward, pushed on by the inertia that defined the institution in the first place. Nine years later, the school again experienced conflict and resignation when the compensation package for the head was seen as extreme.

> "The elite boarding school was searching for leadership in May 2005 when ********* was offered its top job, then for one year. Former ************, an ***********, had retired after the state scrutinized his $500,000 salary and use of school funds at country and yacht clubs. Nine years earlier, the previous head had resigned following a no-confidence vote by faculty. Worth more than a half-million dollars, this package certainly affected the well being of the school." ************ *March 6, 2010*

In the healthiest of schools, the head of school is a visionary who takes a good school and makes it better through the power of her will, her strong sense of values, and her ability to bond people together in a mission. The schools regarded as the finest in the country are schools that try to do just that each time they face the daunting task of choosing a leader. They offer the position to the individual that they believe understands the core values of the school and is able to both uphold those values and challenge the faculty and students to participate in that process of renewal and growth. In kind, the students and faculty unite behind this charismatic leader and do their best to insure that the school moves forward. It is the first and perhaps singularly most important sign of a healthy school. Of course, the head of any school may be well grounded in the institution, although this is no longer as likely as it once was. In days past, schools had legendary heads.

Perhaps the most legendary of all was Frank Boyden, who served as Head of Deerfield Academy for sixty-six years. One of the rights of passage at Deerfield involves visiting his grave. Don't hesitate to grab a copy of John McPhee's The Headmaster for an incredibly strong picture of the early development of the modern American boarding school.

Research your schools fully. That research starts with people who know. If you can afford their services, enlist an educational consultant in your search for a boarding school. Visit www.iecaonline.com where there are convenient tools to help you find a consultant in your area. These are people have spent the greater part of their lives researching the nature of boarding schools. Consultants have a stake in matching your child with the best school possible, and will go to great lengths to ensure that your child has a positive experience. If you want to know about a specific school, ask them. They are there to serve you, not the schools.

Even consultants do not come without a caveat, however. As much as they want to serve you well, some consultants are not always fully impartial or informed about all schools. Its natural- if you have sent a child to a boarding school and seen the school fail them, you'll be loath to send a child there again. Many schools teeter on the brink of obsolescence because the consultants know, or believe they know, that the school is not strong.

If you use a consultant, make sure that you confer about why they do not like certain schools. They'll be honest, and you'll be better informed.

Today, the average tenure for a head of school is approximately ten years, give or take a few. If you find yourself looking at a school whose head has been in place for a long period of time, you are looking at an individual who the trustees feel accurately reflects the mission of the school, as well as an individual who has in practice maintained and built the school's standards. Although you may think that this means that a school is therefore "good", you need to look further. An institution with a long-term head may well be in great shape, but the institution might also be content living in mediocrity. Certainly, this is a tough call to make and demands that you take a close look at the faculty of the school, and whether or not they reflect a long-term commitment to excellence. These are of course, details about a head of school that are not out there in a view book for all to see. How can you discover the traits?

One final extremely important point- Boarding schools were once small sheltered environments where heads of school, while acting as point person of the school, also concerned themselves with the day to day financial matters of the school. Often, today's heads juggle school and external concerns. Do not be surprised to discover that the head of school is more of a chief executive officer and the Dean of Academics responsible for the academic life, the Dean of

Students, residential, etc. All report to the head of school, but each adds their unique twist.

What kind of people am I trusting my child to?

At the end on my junior year, I had the misfortune to lose my father. At the very start of the next year, my senior year with all the responsibility of dorm prefect and looming college applications, I was naturally still strongly affected by that loss. The first night, as I walked to dinner, the Headmaster called me into his office. ("I haven't had time to do anything yet!" ran through my mind) He had recently performed the marriage of a well known cartoonist who had "paid" him in framed drawings of his characters. Knowing that my father had enjoyed the cartoonist's work, after a few words about loss, he gestured to the "portraits" and said, "Choose one." S.P.

When boarding school students are polled about the most influential person in their lives, that person is often a boarding school teacher. That's only logical when the odds are that a boarding school teacher is likely to become a surrogate parent for many of the school's students. Heads of School deal with the greater issues. Boarding school teachers take your child to the hospital at night, deal with him when he gets in trouble and give sage advice when the challenges of adolescence demand the wisdom of an adult. Teachers will intervene in a thousand different ways.

Frank Strasburger took me to see the start of the Boston Marathon because it was, after all, just down the road and neither of us had a class. Others will take your child under their wing in moments of emotional distress, such as the untimely dismissal of a close friend. They are the ones who will ask your child the hard questions about drugs and alcohol, and are there to catch them when they fall. Your child will share things with the faculty that they would never tell you. The loss of their virginity or a horrific failing grade will be fodder for conversation with a boarding school teacher.

One night in Sewanee, Tom Bunting arrived on my doorstep to ask if I would take a walk with him. I ducked back inside, grabbed my coat, and we were off into the frigid night. We threw pennies on icy Gunn Lake, listening as they shimmered audibly into the night. We walked the old cinder track, and Tom eventually revealed his topic. This high school sophomore had lost his virginity the night before, and felt that he had thrown something really special away. For the next forty-five minutes, we worked through it and made progress. Unfortunately, Tom left the school that May, only to return years later to take his life. Sensitive children in a boarding school environment are at great risk.

In many ways the teachers at boarding schools fill the parental roles that you have ceded to them. They are the individuals that provide intellectual engagement for your child. Instead of going home at the end of the day, the boarding school teacher will be there after hours to discuss Samuel Beckett at length, and laugh quietly when your child falls asleep from the academic rigor. They are the evening mentors who help with the geometry problem that would have given you fits at home. Your child will thank a boarding school teacher for guidance and friendship offered. On my yearbook page, I gave special thanks to Mr. Engel (my advisor) and my coaches, Misters Large and Clark. The three together filled something of the role that my father would have played had I been at home. Given these basic facts of boarding school life, be sure that when you entrust your child to a school, you can trust that the school has chosen worthy teachers who are worthy of that trust.

Unfortunately, there is no simple way to discern the quality of a faculty. Degrees may be an indication of academic achievement, but they are no indication of the manner of educator and person that your child is about to encounter. The stories are the stuff of legend. In the course of a twenty-five year teaching career, I saw teachers take their lives, saw them arrested and jailed for sexual assault, fired for sexual involvement with a student, and saw them die from addiction to alcohol. This simply means that they are no different from any other individuals. People are imperfect, so boarding schools are imperfect.

21

Every boarding school faculty is as likely to have as many troubled individuals as any business. We hope that their dedication to the lives of children dictates that their actions are far more likely to be supportive than destructive. Certainly, that has been my experience. Yet, that one teacher who breaks the trust placed by students can forever alter your child's life.

Both Andover and Exeter have struggled with nationally covered sex scandals over the course of the last thirty years. Thankfully, these schools were strong enough to survive the dark and troubling actions of these individuals, but consider the effect of their actions on the students. Each of the schools had counseling staffs that were more than ready to deal with these cases, and in fact, the faculty was probably more shaken than the student body. Such is often the case with boarding school faculties. Owing to the small communities of which they are part, an individual's act can affect an entire group, shaking their very beliefs to the core. In such occurrences, the wounded faculty does their best to hold themselves together while working with your child. Thankfully, such occurrences are the exception and not the rule. Most schools do not struggle with such terrible events in the course of a year, or even a lifetime. They will, however, struggle with the reality of life, and your child will not be safe from the effect.

My own cardiac crisis was played in the lives of my students in the classroom and the dorm. I was not there for a week, and then returned to school a wounded individual. I could not work in the classroom for a while after surgery, but my presence in the dorm was almost immediate. I knew that the girls needed to see me and know that I was okay. Therefore, I went through my own healing process in a far more public manner than I would have in a day school.

With the knowledge that the faculty are human, and subject to the same things that each of us struggle with, the question of what makes a great boarding school faculty looms large. As we continue,

we will address the specific qualities that define great faculty—
qualities you can easily see during the course of a visit to the school.
Some will require that you question the admissions people, or
students, and others you will be able to observe in practice.
Whenever possible, try to take the time watching teachers do what
they do. Do not simply concern yourself with the classroom. Watch
them at lunch, on the playing fields, and simply walking around the
campus. They are not hard to spot, and they tell an important story.

What is a triple threat,
and do you have them at your school?

*One Saturday night, we on the "entertainment committee" had worked
hard and late cleaning up the dining hall after the band that had come to
play. So it was about an hour after curfew when I staggered into the
apartment of the dorm master assigned that night to check in, only to see
him, and two other faculty members about half-way through a big bottle
of Gallo wine. I ignored it, but as I left, I said, "Night Tom." to him.
Tom was my Physics teacher that year, and was visibly surprised at my
casualness, out of character for me. The English teacher started up and
said, "What makes you think you can call him by his first name?" "It's
one in the morning." I answered, "I'm Sam, he's Tom, she's Kathy, and
you're Rushdie. Deal with it." And I left, hearing them laugh behind me.
But I had connected on some level with those teachers outside of the
classroom. And that, in turn, improved how I related to them which then
made the classroom a much more comfortable learning place. Not friends,
but not just teacher/student. S.P.*

You can state one thing with absolute certainty about all boarding
school faculties. No matter who the individual, there is no way that
any boarding school faculty member has any sort of quantifiable
training for the job beyond the anecdotal, or the time they spent as
a student or family member. They have likely had some courses in
education (although this is not always true of independent school
teachers) but they have had no courses whatsoever in boarding
school education. The reason is simple.

23

Despite the hundreds of boarding schools in the country, to my knowledge, no college offers any undergraduate manner of direct education for boarding school faculty members. This is a glaring and troubling fact. Why? The task of teaching at a boarding school is an extremely difficult challenge that demands a unique individual. First, teachers are asked to be able to teach. In all likelihood, that is where you will see an individual teacher's strength. Since boarding schools often make their name on their academic credentials, they work hard to hire knowledgeable faculty well-schooled in their field of study.

However, this is not a guarantee. Economics majors will teach Physics, Religion majors teach English — I once taught computer science while holding a degree in Theater and Rhetoric. That does not mean that we do not know our disciplines. Instead, the meaning is found in the unique nature of a boarding school. Along with the basics of teaching, many boarding school teachers are also called on to coach a sport. As a result, if a school is in dire need of a football coach, you may well find a football coach who has a degree in Economics, teaches History, and coaches varsity football. Oh, and one other thing — in addition to this exotic mixture, the same teacher is also called upon to lead a dorm.

Schools call these teachers "triple threats" as they are asked to do these three things. Many schools maintain that this is the ideal model for a boarding school teacher, and I will not argue with that belief. I spent ten years as a triple threat and, I hope, did the job well. This model is just plain hard work.

For an average teacher, this model means that the teacher is never free for any extended period. As a day school teacher, I marveled at the free time I had that was not there before. I could spend time with my kids after school, pursue hobbies, write, and watch my weekly sitcom. As a triple threat, this was not reality. A number of faculty members thrive under this model, but a substantial number cannot deal with the constant pressure, and tend to let one area of their job fall by the wayside.

More often than not, this area is the dorm, arguably the most important area of life in a boarding school. A poorly supervised dorm is a recipe for disaster. If a teacher is more involved with their grading than the work done by their dorm students, your child is unlikely to get the attention that you hoped boarding school would provide. Of paramount importance therefore is that you query the school about how the faculty performs in the dormitory. You can generally tell from the college acceptance record of a school whether or not they are helping their students succeed academically. If the list reads Harvard, Princeton, Bates, Middlebury, UVA, Occidental, Mills, etc., the faculty are clearly succeeding.

Similarly, it is not hard to find out exactly how good the teachers are at coaching. If a school's lacrosse team is uniformly strong, look straight to the teacher. Repeated success is found when coaches are good at what they do. There are no quick answers in the dorm though. The best way to tell how a school's dorm faculty works is not easily done. If you sit on the hall during study hours, you can easily tell if a dorm parent has a clue about running a dorm. Does the dorm parent stay in her study reading, or is she available for students, working with them in the common room and spending time with them during break? An effective triple threat teacher is almost superhuman, able to keep on putting her best foot forward even when the day has been long and hard. Ask the admissions department about their triple threat people, and see what they have to say. They will tell you the stories if the triple-threats are there and functioning well.

I'm still not sure how my late partner Craig did it- he would counsel a kid, correct a paper, and keep an icepack on a bruise created when a JV Tennis player missed the ball and got the coach instead.

How does the school guarantee the quality of education?

My senior year, I ended up in "realism & naturalism" for English. Not my favorite genre even as an avid reader. But the teacher made the class. We were

25

discussing a passage in one book, by Jack London I think, when the issue of murder came up.

"If you knew you would get away with it, would you kill someone?" Mr. Harvey asked. Asked to a room full of teens who no doubt had entertained such fantasies when angry or upset. We were confused since it wasn't a question any of us had ever been asked to entertain.

"No repercussions," he continued, "Would you do it?" We all looked around uncomfortably, the idea of a potential murderer amongst us disturbing.

"I have." he finished. And that's when we remembered that Mr. Harvey had been a Marine in Vietnam in 1968 and had been in the fighting in the city of Hue during the Tet offensive. And that put a completely different perspective of the whole discussion and brought new understanding to the issues in the book. S.P.

A strong faculty is composed of dynamic, thoughtful, passionate, creative, diverse individuals whose education is ongoing—they see themselves as part of the learning process, and understand that they are both teacher, and still student. . That development can take a number of forms, and it does not hurt to know what manner of developmental choices exist for educators. The clearest evidence of ongoing development is the achievement of advanced degrees in the field that the teacher studies. However, the advanced degree is a little misleading.

Without question, advanced degrees are indicators of scholarly desire and advanced knowledge. Think about it though- the information that a high school teacher actually teaches is information that an individual should have learned in high school. A teacher's advanced knowledge of Russian History is certainly valuable, but not necessarily a prerequisite for effective teaching. Many, many teachers do their job extremely effectively without advanced degrees. One particular teacher I know only has a B.A., yet is widely regarded as an extraordinary scholar in his field. Degrees do not mean everything.

Moreover, if those degrees came to the teacher before she headed to the classroom, they can mean less. A Ph. D. is validation of academic excellence, not of the ability to teach the subject. True, that degree often comes with years as a teaching assistant, but beware the school that hires based first on degree. Workshops though, can go a long way toward filling the holes in a boarding school teacher's training. The Association of Boarding Schools offers important residential life workshops, and there are many other programs that aid teachers in earning a greater understanding of working with children in a boarding school environment. If a school dedicates financial outlay to this type of training, assume that they put emphasis on the student's well-being. This type of training does not end up in a school's literature, but a well-schooled admissions officer will know.

Many boarding schools send one or more faculty members each year to the Stanley King Counseling Workshop, one of the most prominent workshops in the country, training some 100 faculty members a year in "on the fly" counseling skills- skills essential to boarding school faculty. Ask whether or not your intended school sends faculty members to workshops that can make them better residential faculty members. Ask also how they ask those teachers to put those learned skills into play. If they don't, then all the workshops in the world won't make a difference.

Boarding school teachers often come to the profession young and don't get back to school for the Masters right away. Certain grad schools though offer programs that involve intensive and thought-provoking work over a number of summer periods. Given the fact that summer break is one of the great benefits of the business, the teacher who chooses to pursue Masters studies during the summer makes a significant choice. Perhaps more telling is that many of these summer programs do not offer traditional masters degrees. Instead, they offer Masters degrees in "Liberal Studies". This reflects an important fact about the teacher. A teacher that pursues Liberal Studies is one who is going to school for the sake of going to school. They possess a sincere desire to learn more- not just about a specific discipline, but rather a variety of disciplines. Look at the faculty listing and see if there are a few individuals there who have

"B.A., M.A.L.S." behind their name. Seek that person out and you will find a lifelong learner. Since that is what we hope all students will be, that is the kind of faculty member you want to see.

Other forms of training are valuable, and not as easy to discern. Certainly you want to see a record of the faculty at a boarding school having chosen to work with youngsters in a variety of settings. Look at the school's publications, particularly those meant for the alumni body. Remember, when schools write to their alumni body, there is two-fold attack in place. On one hand, they are trying to solicit donations from the alumni body. Without a steady stream of contributions from alumni and parents, poorly endowed boarding schools can fall on hard times with remarkable speed. Their magazines therefore are going to tell you great things about both students and faculty.

A friend and colleague worked on a factory fishing boat off the Alaska coast. At first glance, such a story would appear to have great human-interest value, but little to do with the work of a teacher at a boarding school. I see it far differently. The job my friend worked involved staying up and working for incredibly long shifts, working ungodly hours. He was able to work for hours straight, go to bed, sleep three hours, and then return below deck for another 24 hours of packing fish in ice. Personally, I would not have the stomach to last even a third as long. I would be on the first boat back, except that there was no first boat back. You may not see the applicability of this to the boarding experience, but when he and I had to answer a late-night distress call for a student that involved a 1 AM, 90 minute drive to a city to retrieve a boy from a concert mishap, my friend didn't bat an eyelash. His work in Alaska had prepared him well for the task of staying up all hours to assist a child in an hour of need. That work also prepared him for something else—not yet fluent in the language he was going to teach, he ended up learning Spanish from the men with whom he shared a boat.

Such behavior is not the rule at boarding schools. Often, teachers will take advantage of the first opportunity to hand off that kind of job to an administrator. Instead, Steve followed along and we journeyed to the city to retrieve the child. His somewhat peculiar training made him ideal for the task. This is not to say that you should scour schools looking for Alaskan fishermen. Do however, look for schools whose faculty have unique training that transcends that which you would likely expect from a teacher. Your child will be well rewarded with teachers that bring a unique blend of knowledge to the school experience. Given that boarding schools are unique environments, it takes a unique individual to function within the community.

How can I evaluate the faculty?

Ted Ladd was probably the single most important teacher in my eldest son's life. While Spencer didn't board at St. Andrew's, he might as well have. The campus was his playground, and he grew up looking star-struck at the baseball team. I watched as another father figure came into Spencer's life, and taught him in ways that I never could. He made baseball come alive for my son as not just a passion, but a subject worthy of deeper study. Ted's favorite hitter was Ted Williams. My son's is the same. To this father, he gave more than he knew. Ted's father Fred mowed the grass on the baseball field, Ted worked the infield and taught history at a public high school in the valley below SAS. Faculties are made of all types. G.S.

Experience is a tricky thing to evaluate when looking at the faculty of a boarding school. Often, a school will tell you the most important elements of faculty experience when they print their view book or release information on a website. Beside a faculty member's name, you will often find the year of appointment to the faculty. Without question, those years of appointment are effective tools for your use in determining the commitment level of a school's faculty. If a faculty's years of appointment appear to follow a smooth trend over a great length of time, you are looking at the norm for a good boarding school.

It is only natural that faculty members leave a school. If a school makes consistently good hires, those teachers will be upwardly mobile. Strong faculty members turn into strong administrators, and many school's faculties reflect this natural progression. Indeed, some institutions go this one step further by acting as training grounds for teachers for other schools. Schools that can afford to do use teaching fellow programs to bring a number of young teachers onto their faculties each year. After that year, they are expected to leave those schools and move on to a different experience.

As a result, schools around the country are littered with veterans of the teaching fellow programs- teachers who have worked with extraordinary faculties. Another possible step for these teachers is the natural movement toward graduate school, where they are suddenly valuable candidates who are not only academically prepared to study at the grad school level, but also have the unique benefit of a year's experience teaching in the classroom- a strong benefit when they are selected to work as graduate teaching assistants.

Then, on return to the boarding school workplace, they are armed with three years of teaching experience, an advanced degree, time spent in a boarding environment, and youth. They are likely candidates for triple threat positions, and are extremely well prepared to perform effectively in a boarding environment.

Another manner of experience is extraordinarily rare in boarding schools, and likely the most valuable. Unfortunately, this experience is gained well before a teacher comes to a boarding school, locking out virtually all teachers who have not had this experience in their teens.

What is this piece of magical experience?

Years spent as a student at a boarding school.

Few boarding students go on to choose boarding school as their avocation in adult life. At a recent meeting of the Small Boarding Schools Association, less than twenty out of the more than 200 administrators and educators attending the conference actually had experience as four-year students in boarding school. Why is this experience so valuable? Each discipline that an educator can pursue has an academic program somewhere that can support their search for knowledge. This is not true for boarding school educators.

No one can tell you what it is like to be a boarding student except a boarding student. Moreover, nothing can substitute for that experience. A teacher can be a terrific dorm parent, but if they lack the perspective unique to a boarding student, they are missing one bit of experience that can make the difference between simply working effectively with students and developing relationships with them that make the boarding school experience one of shared mission.

Former boarding students understand the temptations involved in boarding. They understand the difficulty involved in saying no to students who seek to involve your child in the drug or alcohol culture of the school. They understand that balancing the challenging load of boarding school is not simple, and can lend an empathic ear to a student struggling with the complex demands. They are able to see the signs that indicate a student is beginning to fall by the wayside.

Frankly, this list of "things that they can understand" can go on indefinitely. If you have lived through boarding school, you should be able to look clearly into the life of the school and see things that are not immediately visible to individuals who have not been there.

Of course, this brings in another area where you should have a little bit of concern. If you have been a boarding student, then use your experience as well. Take a hard look back at your time in boarding school and compare that to what you believe your child will experience. Despite the passage of time, essential qualities of boarding schools have not changed much. Kids still fight with roommates, still turn on the lights after lights out, still move from room to room when they shouldn't, and generally make choices that ensure that they life they lead is an unhealthy one. If you believe that somehow their experience will be different, you are sorely mistaken.

The exact same things that were at boarding schools in the seventies are there today. Beer, pot, and cocaine have not left, and ecstasy, methamphetamine, and in particular Adderall and Ritalin are now in the mix. Place adolescents in a number of buildings with a number of rules, some well thought out and some seemingly designed to be broken, add a great deal of academic pressure, and troubling behaviors will occur.

An anecdote that captures this quite well is that of the boarding school student in the forties who hid a radio under the floorboards of his room, where there was actually a full-scale environment, complete with chairs and sofas. Each night, the student would go to great lengths to get this apparatus set up and working. The fascinating part? This story was true in 1946, and true in 1976, in the same room at one school. Amazingly, the hatch is still there. How the faculty didn't know is beyond me, and I wonder if that same room is still equipped with a removable piece of flooring that allows parties to go on well into the night hours. Given that there are more than one or two alumni on the faculty, I would hope the trick is no longer a secret, but at some times the solidarity of boarders is such that these secrets remain sacred.

That brings us to the dark side of that experience as a boarder. I went to one boarding school, and worked at different ones. To return to "the old school" is to return to an environment that is so familiar as to bring out qualities in a teacher that were best left behind in high school. What's more, the time spent in a teacher's old school also brings other relationships to bear. No matter how much the student has matured, the ex-boarder in their own school cannot escape the fact the she was a part of that school community in a different role. As such, teachers and administrators left over from that student's boarding school days are likely but unwitting participants in a process that makes the teacher reflect habits and tendencies familiar to all. That can be good or bad, but it is seldom comfortable.

32

The healthiest situation arrives when a former boarder brings their experience to a different school. They are close enough to the boarding experience to remember it well and have clean vision in working with students, but are also functioning in a world that reminds them that they are truly in a different environment. This change is healthy for both the teacher and the students.

Factor in the age of the faculty as well. A strong faculty reflects length of years in service. If you can spend time with an older faculty member, do so. These people are truly the heart of the institution. They have seen thousands of students come and go. The best ones? An elderly curmudgeon from my old school was blessed with a remarkable ability. No matter who you were, or how old you were, or even if this man had you as a student, he knew your name. Without fail, he could identify every student that walked through the doors of the school over a forty-year period. You may chalk it up to a good memory, but to me he is a reflection of a manner of teacher that is rare to find- one that so committed to his work that each child became the focus of his life, both in their years at the school, and beyond. A strong boarding school has more than a few of these characters roaming the halls, turning out lights, and possessing the most valuable experience of all- forty years of life within the walls of the school. While that may lead to a slightly narrow view of life, the students benefit from the loving care of senior faculty members. Pray that the school you select has these characters.

What does it mean for a teacher to be a friend?

The interaction between students and teachers, especially young teachers is complex at best. Adolescents are much the same everywhere, but in such a close environment feelings can go wild. I remember rumors of an affair between a teacher and student. I doubt anything really happened, but the student reveled in the story and did nothing to discount it. And that could have had serious repercussions for the teacher.

But that closeness can also be good. At my lowest during my sophomore year, I was able to go to my adviser's home and just watch some TV, talk about what we were watching and also what I was feeling, and drink a coke. That dose of normalcy helped me get through a very rough patch. And he was able to communicate to my parents what problems I was having so they could reach out more than they might have done. S.P.

One of the longest running questions at boarding schools concerns the relationship between the teachers and students. Boarding schools routinely speak of their faculty-student relationships as both teacher and friend. More than one school video has a student who speaks fondly of the relationship with a certain faculty member as being that of a friend. Having started in the profession as a young teacher, I can heartily emphasize that while the vast majority of these friendships may seem to be positive, there is also a downside to these friendships that may serve as a destructive force in the life of a student. The following examples of relationships are not meant to scare you, or give you pause. They are however, true examples of teacher/student relationships, both positive and negative. Bear in mind also that each relationship is not unique to boarding schools. Children are at risk in public and independent day schools as well. Recent news headlines give ample evidence that adults can misuse a relationship with a student anywhere.

One former colleague has a personal distaste for books that set boarding schools apart because he feels that they unduly separate the normal behaviors of a boarding school from the normal behavior of common society. I agree with him to a degree, but have found that by and large, the relationships between students and faculty in boarding schools are, owing to the constant contact between teacher and student, far more likely to grow into emotionally affecting relationships. Therein lies danger and joy.

The first story is personal, and evidence of an extremely positive faculty-student relationship. As a boarding student thirty years ago, I was struck, along with the rest of the school community, by the sudden suicide of a ninth grade student. Boarding school was not responsible, nor was a student-faculty relationship. If anything, the

34

lack of any connected relationship likely led to this student's choice. The aftermath of that boy's choice echoed in the community for months. In the days following, I was as troubled as anyone, but was helped by the head of school in a unique manner. In any other school, this might never have occurred. During the next weekend, as the school struggled, class and athletics went on as usual.

Students though, could not conduct life as usual. For some reason, still unknown to me, the head of school chose me to be by his side throughout the day. We attended the lacrosse game together, drove up to the baseball game (a ride in car in the 70's was still a special thing) and spent the afternoon together. We did not speak of the lost child, or of the effect on community. We did not need to. The day was one of simple contact between teacher and student, where we shared the unspoken tragedy of the loss. The head and I never spoke of that day in subsequent years, but I am certain that the time we spent together was therapeutic for us both.

Such a moment reflects the positive effect that comes from a normal relationship between teacher and student. All we did was spend time together in a time of loss. Truly, he might as well have been my father in the situation. Student-faculty relationships lead to great things for a school. The late Jay Engel (my boarding school advisor) had an affinity for play going developed into a community wide experience at St. Mark's. To this day St. Mark's students attend an opera production in Boston every year.

In the early days of this program, this teacher shared the theater with a few of his advisees. Over time, the once small gathering grew into a large group of students, finally growing to the point that the entire school became involved in this positive activity. Schools will relate story after story like these to you. They are the meat and potatoes of a boarding school education. Teachers build graduation gifts for students; parents treat teachers to expensive gifts—all in the name of friendship. At St. Andrew's-Sewanee, the year culminates with the presentation of the Annie's—ceramic tokens that come with a bit of prose or poetry written by their advisor.

These people are not lucky. They are simply experiencing one of the most positive aspects of boarding school life. Left alone are the troubling sides of these relationships, and I am almost loathe to bring them to you in print. They are rare, certainly not the norm, but nonetheless a part of boarding school life.

To begin, remember that many boarding school teachers are quite young when they begin their teaching careers. So young in fact that to the students, they more closely resemble peers than adults with responsibility for their welfare. Looking back on my own career, I can remember taking a group of students to a concert when I was all of the tender age of 23. The age range of students must have been between 15 and 19, making up a group that spanned seven years. Given the mistakes I was prone to at that age, I look back on the responsibility endowed with more than a touch of amazement. No doubt, young teachers are also prone to the same manner of temptation that dog teenagers. In many schools, there exists the rumored behavior of teachers with students. Unfortunately, in some cases, those rumors are true. Teachers have smoked pot with kids, shared drinks with kids, and been sexually active with kids.

This is not a characteristic of all teachers or all kids, but a precious few keep this stereotype alive. Alive it is though, and you had best be aware that the behavior, or at least the threat of it, is there. Strong schools make a solid effort to train their young teachers in a manner that helps them understand that the lines between students and faculty must be strictly drawn, not blurred by friendship with students. Young teachers are educated that students are not friends. Instead, they are shown that their role is that of mentor to the child.

They can indeed be friendly, but the faculty must understand that the lines must not be crossed under any circumstance. When they do not, dangerous behaviors can be the result. Check with the school of your interest and see what kind of support systems they have in place for young faculty. Do they have a mentor program? A buddy program of some sort? If they do not, the school is not addressing what should be a major concern.

Look carefully at the qualifications of dorm faculty. Some schools hire dorm counselors with the specific intent that these individuals will function in the dorm, not in the academic life of the school. They become then somewhat like tutors/residence counselors. Whether or not this is a good model is a matter of opinion. If a school hires these individuals based on concrete credentials like degrees in psychology or counseling, you can rest assured that your student's dorm counselor is at the very least aware of many adolescent issues, and probably well prepared to at least listen to your child when the going gets tough. Look out for the dorm counselor who chosen primarily because their spouse is employed by the institution. No one is less likely to have a sense of vocation than the reluctant spouse performing the job simply in order to bring extra cash into the house. Key on the word reluctant though, and remember that for every case where a stereotype rings true, there is a guarantee that the opposite will also hold true. Through the history of boarding schools, many a faculty wife has proven to be the dorm parent that provides young men and women with nurture at a time in their lives where they think it may not be necessary, but is needed anyway. Look too for the teacher who works in the dorm but has little or no interest in the dorm life. If they shut the door to the children with a resounding thud, then the students know that the hall is theirs' from 11:00 on. That is a dangerous situation. Far better is the teacher with a true sense of vocation in the dorm who has morning time freed in order to allow her to be on the floor later than usual in many boarding schools. Ask questions and find out what you must know.

Don't the teachers live in a glass bowl?

The teacher who coached one sport was rumored to be gay and enjoy the physical play. Was he? Doubt it, but that story ran all through my time there. When a divorce happened, the rumor went around that she had left him for another woman. Did she? No. But the closeness of faculty and students in a small area lead to all sorts of foolishness as the "non-work" lives of the teachers were happening so close to the students. Many times when I went to check-in at the end of a Saturday night, the poor dorm parents were consoling themselves with wine/beer with other sympathetic faculty members. And relationships that happened between faculty were very out in the open. When one teacher was seen walking back to her dorm in the same clothes as the night before, we all knew where she had been and with whom (they are married now, I believe). S.P.

Yet another measure of the faculty of a boarding school is their own behavior. This is truly a touchy subject when it comes to discussing a faculty. The problem is simple.

For most people, a separation exists between their working and personal lives. Boarding schools change the rules altogether. A faculty member at a boarding school is forced to live out his or her life in full view of a community. Imagine for a moment that you work for a law firm and your home was suddenly plunked down in the center of the office. If you step outside, all of your employees can see you, and each bit of your behavior is scrutinized. That reality faces a boarding school teacher every day.

No matter what faculty might think, the students notice everything. The result is a group of people who live within a fishbowl, and in most cases, keep afloat. Some though, fail to model actions that students should see. Instead, they will live their life as if students were not in the vicinity. This is a perfect recipe for mixed messages. Take the young faculty member. These days, a youthful faculty member may only be between 21 and 23 years of age. If they have carefully followed the laws of the state about alcohol consumption, drinking is still a relatively new adventure for them. Downing a six pack (or a case) with a few friends is now legal, and a right that the younger faculty will exercise.

However natural, students will observe these actions. Too many young teachers drink, drive and then walk into a dorm. The message sent is clear. Once you have reached a certain age, certain behaviors are acceptable. A school cannot support such action. To do so is akin to hanging a sign in front of the students saying that alcohol abuse is acceptable. Even if we feel that a drunken evening with a designated driver is reasonable, no one can deny that alcohol consumption to excess is simply not good for you. It may well be fun, but it is not good for you.

Students know that fact. Students will tell you which faculty member drinks too much, which one yells at her kids, and which one kicks the dog when she is angry. Your child will return from boarding school able to tell you more about the private lives of the faculty than you want to know. The pressure placed on a school's faculty extraordinary. Hopefully they respond to the added pressure as they should. Students cannot smell alcohol on their breath because faculties are wise enough to keep that smell far away from the students. Truth be told, faculty should actually live a sober life when school is in session. If, as schools advertise, faculty have to be on duty 24/7, then that means that they are sober and prepared to work all the time. Is that a realistic demand?

No, and few faculty members can live up to it. They will be found relaxing with a beer, or caught sneaking a cigarette. Schools need to support these faculty members, so another good interview question might be to ask how the school helps faculty members deal with the extraordinary pressure that they face. Schools will often go to great lengths to allow teachers down time. They will get administrators in the dorm to relieve busy teachers, or sponsor trips out to give teachers a meal away from the dining hall.

They should also be part of the consistent education of boarding faculty that tells them their private behavior must be seen as public. The faculty must behave in the way that they demand students behave. Sober, thoughtful, considerate and open are qualities that any faculty should embody both night and day. Living as an example involves an extraordinary balancing act. Check with other students' families about the faculty outside the classroom hours. If they know too much, then the faculty is far too visible in their actions that show students what is and what is not justifiable.

What kind of teacher am I likely to find?

The teachers I had at boarding school were the usual mixed bag anyone can expect in secondary school. None were bad, given the nature of the institution, but their approaches were quite different. There was the art teacher who would drop a suggestion on me about my pottery, and then

39

leave me alone for two weeks to follow it up. Not every student would make the effort in that case, but he could tell who they were and leave the ones who would alone. It seems odd to say, but being left alone by the teacher in this case taught me more about the medium and my use of it than micromanaging would have.

Then there was the math teacher who recognized my problems with pre-calculus and actually would eat lunch with me to discuss what glad been done in class and what my misunderstandings were.

These are the teachers you hope for. S.P.

Certainly, one of the central reasons that you have chosen to send your child to boarding school has a great deal to do with his academic life. If he was extremely successful in school, you are looking for a challenge. If not, you are looking for the magic that will jump-start your child's academic career. Unquestionably, boarding schools have reason to be proud of the academic qualifications of their teachers.

One of the great perquisites of teaching at a boarding school is the general academic freedom that a teacher receives in planning and executing classes. There is no school board, no superintendent, and often, the department chair will not even tell a teacher exactly what to teach. For individuals who have spent a great deal of time in the classroom as learners, this freedom is often the reason they stay in boarding schools or independent education. As a result, your child is often likely to find teachers who are independent, thoughtful and motivated to do their job in the first place. The following is in opposition to earlier words in this book, but still true.

One measure of the academic qualities of the teacher is certainly to go straight to the school's website and check out the degrees. Heads of school go to great lengths to ensure that their faculty members have at least two degrees. This is one of those places where you can check the degree with a bit of faith. The level of the school a teacher attended may say nothing about him, but the name Harvard, or Yale, or Wesleyan still means a great deal. You can get a great education anywhere, but you do not get in the door at the top institutions unless you have the academic credentials to get in. This is particularly true with graduate schools.

Look for the snobby label. It is okay. Do not however, count on it. In my undergraduate days, I had a professor of astronomy whose academic credentials were impeccable. He was Berkeley through and through, from B.S. to Ph. D. but he could not teach even a bit. I suppose that should be amended a little- he could teach, but more likely, those who could function on the same academic level were going to get the full benefit of his schooling.

The greater concern centers around a simple question- "Can a well-educated person effectively communicate with students on a basic level?" That is the measure of a good secondary school teacher. They teach students not only the material, but also the methods by which an academic must pursue education. Teachers teach kids to think and foster in them a desire for learning. That ability is not taught just anywhere. Still if you can find the same two qualities in a single individual, you have a tremendous teacher.

To see if the teachers can teach, see if you can visit a class. Do not let the visitor simply be your child either. A one-day visit from a child into a classroom does little for the child. How can it? The teacher does not know the child, does not include them, and the child is unlikely to have the ability to judge what actually happens in the classroom. Is the teacher funny and wise, or just prone to making bad jokes? Is the teacher boring, or simply, and obviously, exhausted from the night before? Visiting the class gives you one other chance. You are able to actually talk to the teacher.

At least one school, and probably many more, has taken to having teachers lead tours around campus for families. There is much to be said for the practice. You will know quite easily if the teacher believes in the school, and if the teacher has the ability to communicate that belief. Ask her about the other teachers. In the boarding school world, teachers know the qualifications of the others well—they have seen the awards and positive growth. Ask them to tell about two teachers who do extraordinary things. If they

41

are forced to think hard, worry. If not, rest assured that the faculty is sound and seemingly well prepared to do the job asked of them. There are no guarantees, but examining their life as scholars gives you a snapshot of the scholar they will expect your child to be. The product of the school is an amalgam of the teachers that delivered knowledge, if the base of the amalgam is solid, so too will be your child's growth.

How does the school ensure the safety of the student body?

Hazing sucks, especially if the student does not know how to respond to it. My first year (sophomore) at my school, during the first real snow fall and resulting snowball fight, I suddenly found myself surrounded by the "cool" clique of boys who had already made it clear that I was considered entertainment. I was new, and not really socially up to speed with these "sophisticates".

White-washing refers to when a person is…vigorously rubbed with snow over the entire body and under the clothes wherever possible. It is not comfortable. Given the lack of non-academic things to do (TV was limited to a specific room and times back then), this sort of thing, called "abuse" by the victims and "playing around" by the perpetrators, becomes unfortunately common.

To make matters worse, my roommate, seeking to join the in-crowd, complained to the dorm master on my behalf and then pointed to me when punishment was brought to the white-washers, causing even more problems for me while allowing him to gain some credit for "putting up" with a scrub like me, furthering the casual harassment I could expect. In response, I ended up withdrawing from all but a few close friends. S.P.

More times than I can remember, I have heard students accuse "the school" of doing astonishing things. Students seldom realize that in condemning the school, they often condemn themselves. Remember, the school, although defined in small part by the faculty, is also largely defined by the student body.

42

The knowledge that schools turn over a large percentage of students each year, with a substantial portion lost to graduation, dismissal or exit by choice, is essential in developing knowledge of a school's true community. The fact is that boarding schools, seemingly the same from one year to next, make a substantive change each year. Always fascinating is the view of a senior commencing to college. They look back at the younger students with the honest belief that the school has changed since they arrived. Of course, it has.

The school no longer has the guidance of the older kids present when a freshman arrived. Instead, they are now the leaders of the community, and not prone to think of themselves as keepers of the flame. That influx of new students makes the challenge of keeping schools the same difficult. Admissions officers work hard to find the right student for a school, and this is where you and your child become important parts of the process.

As the admissions committee rebuilds, they search for individuals that maintain the sense of community that school has labored to create. Seldom do they fully succeed. Each year they lose students, and each year they ask some to leave. No matter how hard they try, a school cannot pick an incoming group perfectly. The variables are far too many to allow a school to make the perfect choice every time. If you are unlucky, that wrong choice ends up as your child's roommate.

The first defining factor in a student body is the age of the students. Ideally, the school's classes move upward in numbers with predictable regularity. This is another accurate measure of a healthy school. Year after year, students arrive in shrinking numbers at higher-grade levels. More than a few boarding schools actually discourage or refuse inquiries from students entering their twelfth grade year. By that point, the school knows that each class is filled to an optimal number, and they do not need to go after more students for the sake of filling beds.

That practice is left to the less selective boarding schools. Prestige carries the day in boarding schools; the most renowned schools skim the cream off the top, and the others fight after the crumbs left after the admissions feast of the prominent schools. Given current demographic statistics, the prominent boarding schools are likely to fill with ninth graders relatively early. In fact, many of them maintain a waiting list for spots at the ninth grade level.

When this is true of a school, you are fully assured that the school's reputation is quite strong. Since reputation and reality often do go hand in hand, you are well advised to pursue one of these highly selective schools if your child needs that type of school experience. When schools are able to fill their freshman class, good things happen. Schools that start with solid numbers generally maintain solid numbers, and the student that your child starts her education with is likely to be the student sitting next to her at commencement four years hence.

Why is this important? Minds grow in fervent atmospheres where intellectual competition is, at the very least, the precursor of lively discourse. One visit to a class at an elite boarding school will give you ample evidence of the truth of this statement. A classroom at a high level school is full of young and headstrong minds that make a classroom akin to a pinball machine. It is a challenging place to thrive for four years.

More importantly, students who share four years together in those classrooms come to know each other's means of discourse so well that the art of academic argument becomes joyous. That is not the sole benefit of a healthy number of kids starting at the ninth grade level. In a school that struggles to fill the freshman class, a student does not have many kids her own age to "hang" with. This situation causes big trouble, in a variety of ways, fast. It should come as no surprise that kids need kids their own age. What can surprise though are the choices made owing to a disparity in age.

Here is how that can play out. First, a great disparity in ages at a school leads to the likelihood of "hazing" behind the walls. Hazing takes a number of forms, but each of those forms reflects the same thing — cruelty toward the children in a boarding school setting.

For those of you who need to understand it well, here are some actual hazing incidents from a variety of schools.

#1. A young, pre-pubescent boy finds himself pulled out of the dorm and into the quadrangle of the campus on a winter night in only his underwear. The doors are locked behind him.

#2. Another student is locked into his room with no way out except through a doorway covered with shaving cream.

#3. A student physically attacked by three other boys at 3 AM for his supposed involvement in a discipline incident.

#4. A girl mercilessly teased by students for her adherence to the rules of the school until she finally leaves owing to the ridicule.

That's four. Actual events are often more shocking and sobering. I have paid special attention to this issue because it is exactly the sort of problem that does not generally occur in the home environment. Family members will play tricks on each other, but seldom do you see the manner of behavior that the shrouded culture of a boarding school allows.

Without variation, this type of behavior is visited on those who are least able to deal with the behavior. I've seen children who were taken out of public schools and sent to boarding school because of for the promise of a school environment where hazing would not be a problem.

Not a single admissions officer is going to admit that hazing is a part of the school culture. Indeed, hazing was a part of the culture for so many years at so many years that alumni often look back on incidents of hazing with a fond eye. I can recall the incident of a large water balloon consisting of a condom filled with a copious amount of water that landed in the center of my third form (ninth grade) single.

I can chuckle about the incident only because, in some great cosmic

45

moment of revenge, the balloon failed to break. Rather, it sat on the floor for a long time, simply jiggling like a huge mass of gelatin. When dropped from my third story window, it spread its contents halfway across the quadrangle. Had it done so in my room, the balloon might have been the thing that ended my boarding school career. Repeated incidents of hazing can do just that.

Another problem comes with age differences. Schools that lack a critical mass of any given grade are compelled to place students in dorms where students differ greatly in age. Sometimes you have a senior living on the same hall with a freshman. In the days of senior prefects, this was fine. The senior was a steadying influence on the hall. Although I have not studied this aspect of schools, I am certain that more than a few senior prefects still dominate. They are important parts of the school culture, and should be there.

When you add in more seniors and juniors you bring a completely different mindset into a dorm of slightly post-pubescent children, and lay the groundwork for trouble. Upperclassmen stay up later. They have to. No matter what a school tells you, the upperclassmen are going to be up late in the dorm. For a fifteen year-old girl, the attraction of an older girl's room is palpable. In some cases, schools will even go so far as to room a ninth grade student with a senior. That school has guaranteed that the younger child will be distracted by the life of the senior child. There is no excuse, and the practice cannot be considered healthy.

If the school you are considering believes that such arrangements are healthy, turn the other way quickly. Some school, somewhere, will have a more insightful view of exactly how children should be paired. Generally, there should be no more than a year's gap between students. If at all possible, students who are chronologically similar in age should also cross that gap. The wider the developmental gap between roommates, the more dangerous the situation. If you find you child in such a situation, make a request for a change early and patiently persist. You understand that such relationships can be detrimental, and only you will try to make that change.

Developmental questions are of great importance. It's no surprise to find a ninth grade boy who has not yet crossed through puberty rooming with a child who has already started shaving. Such a child is an unwitting target for the older, savvier child. Often, the only weaponry the child has is wit. More than one small child has developed a cutting sense of humor in order to protect himself from the taunts of the older and wiser. They should not have to do so. A personal defense system should not be necessary in a school environment. Moreover, that defense system may or may not be enough when faced with a child who is ready to attack.

Strong schools have rooming policies in place that protect that younger child. Check and see if you school has such protections in place. If not, be solidly aware that despite the good intentions of the faculty, your child is risk from hazing from other kids that could ultimately derail your child's academic career. This problem is magnified when the reason your child is in boarding school in the first place is to revive a moribund academic career. Hazing and peer pressure from older students will lead your child down an unhealthy path; as a means of building financial strength and athletic prowess, some schools fill their population with postgraduate students. At one time, these students represented an interesting risk within the community. Many years ago when the drinking age in most places was all of eighteen, nineteen-year old PGs were unique creatures.

Why are they there? Scratch a PG and you will often find a strong athlete — one who can really help the basketball team to prominence in the short term. In point of fact, the recent coach of a major college basketball team made his name coaching at Northeast boarding school, a school known for recruiting elite college athletes who need to focus on their studies before admittance to a selective school. Say what you like but the universities do indeed try to admit students who will meet the academic standards of the community. Boarding schools fill the academic void by educating these students and getting a few solid athletes in the bargain.

PGs are not particularly good at helping the school maintain a steady path. Schools want four-year boarders for more than one reason. They bring a steady financial flow to the school, but they also develop a care for the school over a four-year period. Even four year students who are less than positive about their entire experience will someday look back fondly. The PG though may be unable to escape the feeling that he or she is a hired gun for the athletic department — a sense that the school's long-term students will often impress on the PG. As such, the PG can be viewed by the long-term students as a lesser citizen someone who went to school there, but not before he could be of use to the school.

The elite prep school bunch is an exclusive crowd, and PGs are not always invited to the party, unless they can get the tools to party WITH. PGs are not limited to that role however. Many students whose scholastic academic year was not perfect seek to improve their performance by taking a PG year at a boarding school. The hope, often realized, is that the year at boarding school will serve to help the student's grades, and supply a dose of academic reality that four years of high school didn't bring home. As such, the PG is a troublesome character. That is not to say they have to be so.

Some PGs enter an institution looking for a second chance and take full advantage of everything the school has to offer. Their maturity can prove to be a stabilizing force. As a result, the school profits greatly. Still, while their presence may be a positive force, the fact that these students are those who would under other circumstances be enrolled college can make trouble for a school. I've worked with a fair number of PGs. Certain rules are a challenge for them. I ran into more than one PG who told me "I would be drinking if I was at college, so I don't see what's wrong with doing it here."

Students at a boarding school for a single year or less can also disrupt the way things work in a residential situation. There are a variety of reasons that a child will do one year. For some, it is that PG year. Parents will send a child to a boarding school for a year to fix a problem, or make it more convenient for them to do what they want. Still others decide early on in their boarding school career that they are going to leave at the end of the year, and that there is nothing that the school can do to stop them. There is no more dangerous student than the careless one year "body." Ultimately, this student is extraordinarily selfish, does not care if your child is caught up in trouble.

Therefore, while the child who that didn't care is on her way home, your child is home on suspension, dealing with the consequences of her acts, face to face with possible expulsion from school. For students who have tied themselves to the school, that threat of expulsion is either the great wake-up call or the beginning of the end. For others, it's tacit approval to do whatever they like. Worse, they really do not care whom they bring down with them. When it comes to anyone else's self-interest, they simply turn away.

If then, the school that you are looking at seems to have a large population of students that stay there for only a year or so, question them hard as to why. I am certain that this can make sense as a policy decision but it is a survival tactic. Some boarding schools will turn down a one-year boarder in March that they will accept in August if the beds are not full. Certainly, there are a number of fine schools that have waiting lists that fill their beds well before the end of the school year. The ones that do not are digging late into the summer, and indeed, often the school year itself. The one-year border is a convenient way to fill beds, but an inconvenient way to build a boarding school community.

You wouldn't believe this possible, but it's true. At least one school I know admitted a nineteen-year old PG on the day school began. He arrived with his suitcases for his interview, and his father's checkbook had a sufficient balance. After admission was granted, the student lasted all of a month before expulsion for repeated use of racial slurs. For my friends that were at that school for the year, this boy's expulsion was simply the beginning of a long year.

If a school will take your child on the spot, take time to think. Someone has to. Find an admissions director from any boarding school, and ask her exactly how many four-year boarders she would like to admit each year. You will rapidly discover the worst kept secret in the business. While the business of education in most schools is concerned with the shaping of an adolescent's mind, the admissions department is looking for a four-year boarder,

49

preferably full pay, not scholarship.

If you and your child fit into that class, and your child has enough strength to propel a hockey puck at an extremely high rate of speed, they want your child. Why? First, by their third year, four-year boarders know the school community as well as anyone, including the faculty and head of school. They know the maintenance people that look the other way at night, and the kitchen worker who will give them extra food if they ask in the right way. They know every bit of school history from the past years, and can tell legendary stories of this party, this near-escape, and in particular, how the school really runs. The four-year boarders know both the world of the faculty (or so they think) and the world of the student. They reside near the heart of the school and provide the leadership that is required of a senior class. That leadership may be negative (worst case scenario) but it will be there.

A school limited in its ability to attract four-year boarders is also limited in its ability to attract students and families who buy into a school for an extended period. Failing to do so, the community fails to deliver on some of its core promises. What keeps a four-year boarder away from a school? By and large, reputation. A school that has a long history of students attending for four years (or even in the old days, five and six years) will continue to see a line of students approaching at the ninth grade year. The societal expectation calls for four years, and for four years, they will come. If not, there are serious questions that must be raised.

This is not to say that many schools that pull students for a three-year tenure are weaker in nature. Nothing could be further from the truth. There is though a reason that the kids did not show up in their freshman year, when students are accustomed to making the break. For some, the defining element has been the general societal change from public and private junior high schools, with their traditional two year track, to middle schools that run on a three to four year track. This manner of schooling has made deep cuts into the boarding school applicant pool, and only the strongest of schools keep a steady stream of four-year boarders.

Schools have downsized to reflect this demographic trend, while others learned that it pays to staff admissions offices with a number of people proportionate to the job. Perhaps in the fifties, when only elite students headed for the elite schools, one man could handle an admissions office. Now, with the demands of multicultural recruiting, the need for boarding schools to open up new markets and the pronounced competition between schools for students, the stakes are raised. It is not unusual to see a boarding school trying to fill about 130-150 beds per year with a staff of five to eight admissions people. One travels (usually to the Far East or Saudi Arabia), another sets up parties in target areas (led by parents) and others stay home, crunch numbers, and try to admit a group of students they believe represent the ethos and character of the school.

As the parent of a rising ninth grader, you are akin to gold to these institutions. Your child has an enormous advantage over other applicants, and can expect to see more generous financial aid offers, more contact with the school, and an overall sense that the school sincerely wants you as much as you might want it. The dance performed for prospective four year boarders is seductive and worthwhile. Enjoy it.

What do you do about sexuality?

My school once had no locks on the dorm doors, due to the expected observation of the honor code the students signed. This was not a good situation in a coed school. I have often wondered if it was a stolen laptop that changed that policy or someone reported a sexual assault and made it stick. One can be concealed from parents, one cannot. Strong leadership by faculty and staff will not stop sex from happening in boarding schools, but it can make sure it is not harmful. S.P.

I'll not go into depth about how Teenagers are sexually active in ways not common 30 years ago.

So how do boarding schools deal with that fact? Just like the rest of society. For the most part, faculty members wish that the question

51

of sexuality didn't crop up too much. Just as it is a difficult topic for a parent to broach, teachers don't have a walk in the park with it either. And there's the rub.

Make no mistake about it, schools worry about sex, but I've seen few that are preemptive about human sexuality issues. When I think back on my career as a dorm counselor, I'm a bit ashamed of the things that I missed over the years. The girls in my dorm (not all) were out there having sex, and the boys in my dorm were doing the same. We just didn't talk about it much until disaster struck. And disaster did strike.

Just as in the society outside the walls, I've been witness from near and far to a vast number of disastrous moments. STD's, Date Rape, Rape, suspected pregnancies, actual pregnancies- you can continue this list by yourself. These are tough issues for schools, and are kept behind the walls unless something happens that is so egregious as to draw the attention of the outside world. So, your child will have to process the experience without your help.

In a way, this may be a positive for schools. Kids are often far more willing to talk about sexuality issues with an adult that is not their parent. You might recall that Tom Bunting came to me simply to talk about the fact that he had lost his virginity the night before. He was heartbroken because he realized that he had experienced a powerful moment with the wrong person. As we walked about the lake, he expressed his guilt, his new found knowledge, and generally used me as someone to process the experience through. I was honored, and he was finally wiser, though deeply affected by the experience. So yes, remember that sex is going to happen, and that boarding schools are not going to stop it from happening, no matter how hard they try. It was true in 1974 and it's true today. And given what I've learned in life, it happened a lot longer ago too.

I can't go further though without reflecting on something my sons revealed to me. In today's sexual culture, they tell me, we are seeing a huge shift. More and more, "hooking up" is becoming a part of the standard of sexuality, and young people with several partners are not unusual. It's not my job to detail what's happening, but I

52

thought you might like to know. It's a discussion to have before anybody goes to boarding school (or walks out the door in the morning).

Another major issue confronts boarding schools that few are strong enough to fully embrace. When you consider that adolescence is the time when children are learning about their own sexual identities in the first place, imagine the child struggling with sexual identity. Strong schools tackle the questions of human development with ardor. Throughout a certain breed of school, gay and straight alliances have surfaced in spite of the prejudice that still prevails. Like it or not, gay children in boarding schools must confront a load of issues. An openly gay child at boarding school is a rarity. Friends will know, but the culture is such that widespread acceptance is not likely to be forthcoming.

If your child is gay, be so forward as to ask the school about their policies. They cannot discriminate in admissions, but their community ethic may make it impossible for your child to survive and thrive in that school. An honest admissions officer will understand the issues well enough to give you adequate guidance in this area.

On your own, you can still look for the obvious signs of an accepting community. Are there openly gay faculty members? Does the school promote gay partnerships? Do they go so far as to accept gay faculty members cohabiting on campus with their partners? If so, your child will be accepted in the community, and able to move through adolescence with support, no matter her sexual orientation.

If the school appears less than accepting, don't lose heart. Ask during your visit if there are other parents that you can talk to about the school experience. They may well be forthcoming in ways that the school cannot. Remember that this simply isn't an easy topic to address. Schools with a religious orientation are bound by dogma. They say one thing, but on the other hand acknowledge that sexually active kids are on campus. After all, what can they do? In a time when condoms are advertised on television, and blatant

53

sexuality is used to sell everything from tires to coffee, kids are going to get the message that it's okay. That's why a school should make its policies clear. They must have mechanisms in place for issues of sexuality, and be prepared to deal with potential problems. No mechanism though is a substitute for solid preemptive counseling for boarders. As difficult as it is to talk about, boarding schools have to. If they don't your child will float in a sea of suggestive sexual messages that all say "Do it!" That's not good for any child.

What happens when someone doesn't fit in?

One of my classmates was of a very…artistic nature. He was also one of the in-crowd, not only in my class, but among the older students, too. He was "edgy" and "hip" and too cool for school. And he was disturbed.

After his repeated bullying of classmates and disrespect to staff came home to roost, expulsion raised its head. A senior organized an art show of this boy's work and petitioned the administration to keep him on, pointing to his great artistic potential and painting him as just misunderstood.

One week after he had been put on probation, he appeared on dress-up day (Halloween) as breakfast: smeared with butter, cream cheese, cinnamon, eggs and toast. He was promptly expelled that day. I hope he got the counseling he needed. S.P.

Schools don't talk about the black sheep. Your school will seemingly guarantee that the student your child will live with, or adjacent to, will be much like them. If not, the roommate will be from a culture that enables your child to both live and learn. Largely this is true. They will try.

Nevertheless, be forewarned they will fail as well. For every perfect living situation that a harried Dean of Students creates, she also just plain misses it more than her fair share of times. Your child may come to school with great racial pride, and find his roommate has a flag on the wall that can be considered racially inflammatory. Your daughter's roommate, who seemed so nice, just happens to suffer from bulimia, prompting many a scared call from your child. Worst case scenario? Your child becomes aware that his roommate is considering taking his own life. This happens many times, and no school community, or home community, is immune.

These events shake the lives of students, but also are events often swept beneath the carpet until such a time as they represent substantive health and safety issues. Moreover, because kids do not "narc" on each other, they do not tell anyone at school. That is an awfully heavy burden for a child to carry, but carry it she will until someone asks. That is when you have to have the most faith in a school.

Schools working through the normal details of everyday life have generally got things pretty well covered. Faculty members know who is on duty at what time, which kids are sick—all the standard things that they have got to know. Seldom are they well enough informed about the each child's whole life. Often, parents want a child's entrance into boarding school to represent a fresh start—a time and place where a child can get back on track. Unless support systems are completely in place though, success is certainly not a guarantee. Old habits have a way of returning, and boarding schools frequently deal with children who sincerely need counseling.

Again, your school has hopefully put into place faculty and staff trained to identify adolescent issues before the adolescent issues become adult problems. Most though, are imperfect. They cannot always figure out who is going to survive. One former student speaks with me often of the student that he knew was going to use suicide as an option, but this boy could not get anyone to believe his roommate was serious. Rampant drug use and non-functional academics should have made us all completely aware, but we were not. I remember watching, aghast, as the troubled student's advisor used "tough love" on the student, completely forgetting about the love part. Naturally, the student made his suicide attempt (and thankfully failed) but the roommate still thinks about it years later.

He believes the school was wrong in taking this child's actions as merely peculiar and not dangerous. But then, the student was a freshman, a young man at the very beginning of a four-year boarding career. What did he know? Ultimately, he discovered that he knew more than any of us, and still uses the incident as an example of one school's hypocrisy. I strongly believe he is misguided in his attack, but there is certainly a kernel of truth in his accusation.

What is the school's commitment to a diverse community, and how does it address the tension?

Back in the mid-eighties, my boarding school was not very diverse, with the majority of the students from upper-middle class, white backgrounds. My year-book is full of pictures taken on beaches, sailboats, and tennis courts. My class had only two black members, one of whom was from the "tough streets" of the Bronx (as I recall). The "exotic" nature of this guy made him very popular at the school and a leader in cultural fashion. He was, simply, outside of the majority's experience. Exposure to influences like these is important, but their scarcity at the time elevated his "otherness" to Big Man On Campus status, a position he (not surprisingly) enjoyed quite a bit. S.P.

The pastoral image of the New England boarding school is common. So common indeed, that many of you are likely to have the image presented by the media planted firmly in your brain. In "Dead Poet's Society," a classic boarding school film, the campus seemed as if it must be that of a New England boarding school. So familiar in fact, that I stayed to watch the credits, certain I was looking at the campus of a school whose sports fields I had visited long ago. My surprise was palpable when I saw that the prototypical New England boarding school, right down to the snow, could be found in Delaware. So it is with boarding schools.

As many boarding schools that seem to match some manner of norm are complemented by a number that seem a different type of boarding school. Schools exist on the Monterrey peninsula in

56

California, in inner city Tennessee, rural Mississippi and Connecticut (could you imagine more different worlds?) and even for children of distinct racial and cultural backgrounds there are more than enough to match your child's needs. With the location though comes the added dimension of geography—a dimension that can have a great deal to do with your child's success.

In Far and Wide, a girl from the inner city aptly describes her feelings on coming to live at a boarding school. She was accustomed to the city, but her Pennsylvania school was anything but that. In that environment, she was struck by fear-something she had not known in New York. In Lorene Cary's Black Ice, she too speaks of how the rural culture she met as school was foreign to her. Do not underestimate the pain of Lorene Cary's experience if you take the time to read Black Ice.

If you are contemplating boarding school for a child who will bring diversity to the school culture, remember that she is going to settle into a school where her presence itself is part of the marketing of the school. Long ago, children from diverse ethnic backgrounds were unable to break into the world of boarding schools except in rare institutional circumstances. Today, schools want a diverse population, wherever they might come from.

As a result, children end up in strange situations that can bring about conflict between students. I've seen racial incidents in the North and the South. The pressure cooker that is boarding school can make these incidents flare all the more. There's no prescription for avoiding such experiences. The gift of diversity brings the altogether difficult task of bringing children from diverse backgrounds together.

Ask early about how the school deals with cultural diversity. There's no perfect answer to the questions either. You must simply decide whether the school's ethos makes sense to you. Add in the variables of geography, and you will develop an accurate picture of the school your child needs. Where is that school? The rural boarding school is the most common image, with good reason.

Boarding schools were founded to provide an academic life for children of wealthy families from a variety of areas. The rural schools therefore sprung up somewhat distant, but generally within a train or buggy ride's distance from the large eastern cities of Boston, New York, and Philadelphia. This explains why then rural (and now suburban) Massachusetts around Boston is dotted with schools, as are the territories immediately surrounding New York and Philadelphia. The idea was simple. Remove the children from the city, and get them together in an academically challenging environment with a large number of like-minded souls.

The choice to go rural developed a mindset in boarding schools that is as prevalent today than ever. Their students view rural boarding schools, despite the attempts of activity directors to combat this image, as anything but the real world. Of course their world is quite real, but they are withdrawn from a variety of elements of daily life outside boarding schools that make their lives seem remote from reality. Newspapers are not common at schools.

They exist in many classrooms and libraries, but kids do not gravitate toward the local news store to get a paper. In their down time, kids are far more likely to watch "The Simpsons" or play a physical game with their friends. When you are at a rural boarding school, popular culture takes second place. What's more, and probably worse, faculties at rural schools can develop the same narrow focus.

When teaching at boarding school, I frequently took stock of my last few weeks to see how many times I actually left the campus of the school for an extended period of time. I found that my forays into the real world tended to be commercial or health oriented. I either picked up videos or went to the doctor. The golf course also beckoned three times a week on a special membership for faculty members. That certainly does not count as the real world.

With today's advanced technologies, there is probably less concern about the insular nature of according school. Kids get frustrated, but the frustration for the children is temporary and livable. Young boarding students mourn the lack of snow days, but only until lengthy vacations arrive. The same is true with the Saturday classes that still exist at a number of schools. They seem bad at first, but you are there anyway, so why not go to class?

Rural schools have a wide variety of benefits as well. They are distant from the city, which means that students do not have easy access to the temptations that abound in a city environment. They are free to focus on their studies, and have a faculty to support them in that endeavor. The closed community can provide close friendships, closer even than those a student might find in a day school setting.

Students also have the opportunity to discover the wealth of beauty in the surrounding area. The rural nature gives students the great outdoors to explore, use as solace, and simply get out and walk. Safety issues with rural life need to be addressed by whatever school you are examining. Take a good look at their policies regarding the outdoors. There are certainly as many different policies in places there are schools. Institutions have a tendency to react to difficulties by putting structure into place, so their policies, always outlined in the student handbook, are well worth reading. These policies will tell you just how safety-oriented a school is in policy.

Those policies though cannot tell you what the reality is when it comes to students living on a rural campus. Given the presence of wooded areas, kids gravitate toward them for reasons both good and bad. On one hand, the woods are wonderful places to get away from the pressures of school. On the other, they also represent terrific places to disappear and break rules meant to protect the children. As such, you get a fairly lethal combination of unknown territory and judgment impaired kids. That is a recipe for disaster, and many schools are subject to that danger.

Luckily, kids often have enough intelligence to conduct themselves in a safe manner. Frankly, if they are breaking rules, they are even more likely to be careful. Not only do they wish to avoid danger, they wish to avoid getting caught or even seen by adults. Make no mistake though, the woods beckon students at rural boarding

59

schools.

You will be able to tell if the school takes its role in the protection of the children properly by the manner in which they deal with the boundaries of their rural campus. A well-lit rural campus should be no surprise to anyone who knows about the world of boarding schools. The rape of a former colleague brought home the fact that no campus, however rural, is safe from the dark reality of life in this era.

The urban campus brings another problem altogether. When a boarding school is placed within a city, students have a cornucopia of temptation at hand. No matter the rules of the school, students are able to work around the structure and take advantage of everything they can. The healthy school takes care of its student needs with paradoxical controlled freedom. Since students have so much at their behest, schools build a rule structure that allows students the opportunity to taste the good life of the city, all the while protecting the students from the harsher elements. Those elements are truly dangerous.

Look at the many urban universities that dot the landscape of the country. They maintain full time police forces to handle security on campus, and work diligently to keep the campus secure. Urban boarding schools have the same challenge and should react in a similar way. Not to do so is to tempt fate.

At this moment, the student activity director becomes the key player. The task is monumental—devise a plan whereby upwards of 400 adolescents are kept entertained either on or off campus, and protected from the city. This is another of those "ask the student" issues. Students will not hesitate to tell you (or particularly your child) about how weekends work at their school.

A healthy urban school will supply its students with a wide variety of entertainment options on any given weekend. Dances are certainly common, but some schools go so far as to bring name entertainment onto the campus to serve the students. Name entertainment brings another bunch of problems, but at least you know that your children's needs are addressed, and that the school is making a concerted effort to keep the children under their wing.

Things to look out for? More than a few schools will set their children loose on the weekend, allowing them to freely check out into the city. There is not even a question about the danger involved with such a choice. Schools are banking on a simple assumption. They possess the belief that their students are trustworthy and intelligent enough not to make choices that will end up dangerous. Having spent at least one afternoon in Boston's infamous, and now defunct, Combat Zone, I suppose I'm walking evidence of the failure and success of my school.

Yes, I went to a stupid place. No, I did not do anything stupid. Thank God. Remember also that the urban school has more immediate access to the items that make for a tough weekend at boarding school. Alcohol and drugs do not get to boarding schools by themselves, and students do meet friends in the city in order to make exchanges. No school, urban or rural, is exempt from this practice. This act is specific to no school, but common to all. Short of a pat down on return to campus, schools are subject to the possibility that illicit goods will make the short trip from outside the walls to inside the walls.

Worse yet, depending on the staff of the school, the kids don't have to go far at all. More than one employee at a boarding school has been released for supplying kids with alcohol or drugs. Just because they are behind the walls doesn't mean they are safe from the outside. Only a strong school with diligent faculty members can ensure any measure of safety for a child. In the case of some schools, that safety may well exceed the safety at your home. That's when a boarding school truly becomes the most sensible choice you can make for your child.

You must make sure that all of the necessary measures are in effect and working. I'm not telling you to be a nuisance, simply to remember that your child is your child, even when they are not in your home. They still need, and their caregivers need, your guidance. Think of it this way. Would you have ever left a babysitter with your child without explicit instructions for proper care? Boarding schools make the rules, but make sure that they reflect your idea of what represents proper care for your child.

What once were rural schools are now, in many, many cases, suburban. Urban sprawl has had such an effect on boarding schools that many schools are now parts of bedroom communities for the cities they once served from afar. Cars brought everyone closer, and the schools suddenly became the center, and in some cases the major real estate holder in some formerly small towns. I visited one school recently that still had woods out the back door, but the formerly rural campus was now clearly a sanctuary in the midst of urban sprawl.

The effect on schools? With communities springing up around them, boarding schools have seen the growth of the day student population. Schools that once consisted solely of boarding students now have a substantial number of day students. In some cases, the number of day students has actually surpassed the number of boarders. This change is fundamentally important because with the rise of the day student, the demand for space in boarding environments has become less pronounced.

Indeed, is it sensible to pay nearly thirty-five percent more instead of your child at home receiving an equally strong day school education? If the boarding experience is that important, parents will pay. A large number though have chosen to make the town boarding school the town day school as well. Schools struggle with this demographic change. Once accustomed to simply boarding, suddenly they must deal with policing the larger area of the town, and are concerned with exactly how to work with students that sign out to a day student's home. Schools are forced to develop umbrella rule policies that cover who are under what rule when a student signs out.

Again, more than one school has been forced to discipline at least twenty students partying at a day student's home. The presence of suburbia around the school makes the school suburban. As a result, your child may be right back in the environment you were trying to escape. The school may seem rural, but suburbia has a great way of imposing itself upon the life of the school. That is why the school's definition and evenhanded application of the rules to all disciplinary offenses is essential to the health of the school. It is not an easy job. The suburban school may have the toughest job of all. They do not have the remote nature of the country to isolate them, nor the obvious nature of the city to force them into strong security choices.

What kind of freedom (both good and bad) do your students have?

A month before I graduated, we had our annual spring concerts. During this three day period, there was almost no direct supervision of students, nor was there much structure. I looked around at one point, and realized that the three people around me were talking about getting some booze, and looking to me, the only senior, for approval. "We have no cash." I said. Well, yes; the sophomore had fifty on him because his mother had sent it last week (no ATMs back then). "We don't have ID." I tried. Well, yes; the junior had a fake ID that had worked at a local place before. "We can't get there." Well, yes; the other guy should have been a junior, but had left after hazing became too much for him. He had a car.

I gave in. And knowing that the popular kids had been partying all the years I had been there let me rationalize giving in. I wanted to know what it was all about. It was my first drink. S.P.

The academic day at boarding school only comprises about eight hours of your child's life. To be certain, studying is supposed to take up another portion, but reality dictates that students have the option to use those hours in a variety of ways. How they use them has an enormous effect on your child's success or failure in the boarding school world, and their ability, not the school's, to use that time effectively will finally define the result. Here's what life was like about fifty years ago.

The boys at a boarding school would arrive for breakfast and sign in after a long night's sleep. Lights out for the younger boys might have been 9:00 or 9:30, with a graduated schedule for the other students. Seniors would naturally have the most privilege in keeping with their academic demands. After signing in at breakfast, a great number of schools had organized work programs, often put in place during a time of war when help was scarce. Students would do these chores, and then be off to a day of classes.

Halfway through, students would sit for a formal lunch before continuing class. Shortly thereafter, boys would switch into athletic gear and get ready to play a sport. In general, all of the children, athletic or not, were required to play an interscholastic sport. In New England schools, this gave birth to ancient rivalries still in place today. Practices or games took place nearly every day of the week, and students were hard pressed to make it from sports to chapel on time. After chapel (not the rule in all schools) students would sit for dinner, again in coat and tie, and then enjoy a brief respite from schedule until study hours.

There were as many study plans as schools, but all guaranteed some manner of supervision. After studying, students had a brief time to make a phone call, perhaps clean their room or play a game, and then hit the bed before another day arrived.

Certainly there were discipline problems within this structure, and plenty a child was fired from school. So stringent were the rules however those children didn't have the time to play games with the structure. Yes, students in the forties drank beer too, and young people planned and executed elaborate pranks. Thankfully, those were the heights of danger. The system protected them. The rules have changed. We all know that. Societal norms have changed in such a manner that boarding school represents something far different than fifty years ago.

When a child in those days went to school, despite the harsh rule structure, they possessed a certain freedom that made boarding school free of any number of restrictions they may have faced at home. That notion has sailed far away. Today, boarding schools are often considered an alternative when a student needs structure that can't be provided in the home setting. For whatever reason, kids end up at boarding school without the things that they had at home.

The car, and easy access to entertainment, is gone. The friends don't live across town. They are in the room next door, and the parents have been replaced by harsher individuals who demand that you get in bed by 11:00 PM, even if they let their own children stay up into the morning hours. No longer do boarding students feel free. Rather, many feel imprisoned by a rule structure.

Certainly, this is not true at all schools. The measure though, of whether a school is a good fit for your child lies within the rule structure of the school, and how those rules are applied. Here's an example. Let's assume that a school, as its main form of punishment, has a detention system that keeps students from enjoying their free time after supper. If the students understand that this punishment is strong, and will lead to severe consequences if not taken with humility, then the rules should work well.

Watch though, for the school that doesn't have a handle on its rule structure. Without a strong sense of structure, we know that kids will use every bit of freedom allotted to them. If these same children discover that they can get away with missing detention, they will skip. Frequently.

Moreover, if they discover that the school's reaction is to place them on some manner of disciplinary probation, they will work within the structure until they realize that the structure doesn't really mean anything. Woe to you and your child if you place them in such a school.

Beneath the surface of such a school you will discover, if allowed to look, that the students are running the school, not the other way around. That is dangerous. In that world, the students learn to work around the structure and create a dangerous subculture that threatens all students in the environment. Your sweet child who simply needed more structure in her life could be in waters over her head before you know it.

Casualties of Privilege was all about this private world. Unfortunately, that book was created in a time when the societal pressures and the potential dangers were less than they are now.

Even ten years ago, a child would have likely been seen as a pariah if he dared to offer a drug like ecstasy or LSD to an underclassman. Trust a boarder—to do so is the height of foolishness. The immature child likely to screw up is the last person that you offer drugs.

It took until my senior year, in an era of enormous marijuana use, for anyone to actually offer me the opportunity to use drugs. I was not considered safe, and certainly not a part of the culture. Few students are seen in that manner anymore, and if you have a suggestible child, the prospect of drug or alcohol use is there. Older students can and will prey on them.

Louis Crosier's essayists in <u>Casualties of Privilege </u>did an effective job of addressing the subculture of a school, and I risk repetition by detailing that same subculture. Even in Crosier's book though, the full spectrum of that life was not addressed. The central problem is this: when the faculty go to sleep, the students don't. A school will go to great lengths to convince you that they do, but they are not telling the truth.

Boarding students want to stay up later because they are already accustomed to late nights, and will do whatever they can to keep the night alive. If you find this difficult to believe, only anecdotal information will suffice to convince you, so here it is. As a faculty member, I was stunned to discover the length students would go to in order to "party" at boarding school. I assumed, falsely, that once the students FINALLY went to bed, after much cajoling, that they were actually going to sleep. No doubt, they made a great show of going to sleep.

Had I stayed up a few hours later, I would have seen the truth of the after-hours social life. Believe it or not, and I had a hard time believing it, students will actually go to sleep and then rise at odd hours of the morning in order to party. The hour of choice for those I encountered? Four A.M. There was no way that I could suspect that these students would do such a thing because the very concept seemed ridiculous to me. Drugs and alcohol are powerful, but powerful enough to make their intoxication a desired effect in the late hours of the morning? Evidently so.

66

I found it difficult to believe that students would still pursue these avenues. A little bit of thought would have served me well in recent years. Ecstasy and cocaine are present in boarding schools. Had I considered that, perhaps I would have been more concerned about kids staying up all night on the weekends. Former students let me know that indeed, the party didn't start until deep into the night. It didn't matter if the lights were out or not- the party went on.

On the occasion that I stayed up late to check on the kids, I never failed to find that there was action in dorm after lights out. As I think back over the years, that has been a constant in boarding school. No matter where my travels took me, the lights came back on. In point of fact, I used to put boarding schools to the test late at night. Whenever I visited a school, so long as I could get back into the building where I slept, I made a point of going out for a late night walk. I didn't want my sole vision of a school to be that daytime visit where everything was sanitized for my eyes. Most schools didn't disappoint. The lights would pop on late at night as students undertook the activities that started after midnight.

How important are AP courses at your school?

I took no honors or AP courses at my boarding school. I was not so ambitious, and, truth to tell, they seemed to be more about the test and not the material.

But I learned how to learn. With mandatory study hall in my room from 8-10pm, I learned that if I got work done early and got all my required work out of the way, I could settle into the armchair I had scrounged from somewhere with the book I wanted to be reading for far longer. Or continue the ongoing game of hearts that me and my friends had going. And because I was encouraged in that approach, I can learn all I want about any topic. I hate realism/naturalism in American literature, but I know why I don't like it.

Boarding school taught me how to buckle down and do the work as well as I could and as soon as I could, no matter how I felt about the subject, so I could got on to the things I wanted to do. Not everyone learns that particular lesson, but it was the most important one that I could have picked up. And the knowledge I have picked up with that trick? Priceless. S.P.

More likely than not, you send your child to boarding school for the sake of the academic program. Because each boarding school is an independent school, there is little in place to actually ensure that a school's academic program is effective. The various accrediting boards do an admirable job, but their job is extremely specific in nature. They are not there to decide whether the school is a "good" school by their own standards. I'm sure that many accreditation visitors have been appalled by the beliefs of some schools.

However, they visit a school to discover exactly how well a school knows itself, understands its policies and practices, and then puts those policies into action effectively. Specifically they aid the schools in achieving their missions, and are there to tell a school if they have strayed far from their mission and fail to execute the work they have set out to do. They are not there to make judgments on faculty members, courses as taught in the classroom, the way a team is coached or even the way a dorm counselor will speak with your child.

To their credit, I am certain that this is a great concern to ac-creditors, but they cannot go in and try to change a school's ethos. If a school has decided, by design, to admit only girls, house them in singles, and teach them one class at a time for six week periods, the ac-creditors accept that is the mission of the school, and then work with the school to identify areas in which they succeed or fail. Almost by default, schools that you examine are likely to have all of the proper accreditation in place. The process assures that schools do a substantial self-evaluation that nearly guarantees accreditation. Some schools will have multiple accreditations from different sources. These represent a substantial effort on behalf of the institution to look carefully at its work.

You must decide if the school's mission is an accurate match for your child, and whether what you see in present practice is actually

68

worthwhile. There are no standards that define whether or not a school's mission is misdirected- only if they succeed in reaching their goals.

Many schools offer AP courses as a means of preparing students for college and defining the rigor of the academic program. If you are not aware of the AP program, here is a brief primer. AP courses, more accurately known as Advanced Placement courses, are designed to give high school students college credit for their work. At the end of a year of study, schools administer standardized exams, and colleges may offer credit to students based on the scores on these exams. In principle, AP courses appear to be an excellent investment in your child's education, and many boarding schools offer strong AP programs. These programs though are delivered to students while national debate takes place on the courses and exams themselves. A few paragraphs are insufficient to adequately explore AP courses. Let the following suffice- if you choose a boarding school based largely on the nature of its AP program make certain that you ask the proper questions.

Does the school have quantifiable evidence that the courses as offered actually produce college credit? Is there evidence to support that the classroom experience is centered on learning the material for knowledge's sake and not simply to pass a test? These questions will tell you much about a school. With honors programs at the finest boarding schools (and probably the poorest) the word "honors" is rarely spoken. The standard is simple- at elite academic boarding schools, the need for specific AP courses is not pronounced. The reason for this choice is simple. Students at academically ambitious schools take classes that are already adequate preparation for AP exams. Specialized study in the manner of thought and dedication necessary to receive college credit for high school work is already in place. The truth be told, many classes at elite schools are of such quality that they will already challenge students at many colleges across the country.

The stringent demands of instructors at these schools are legendary. As a natural byproduct, their students will be more than adequately prepared for almost anything that the AP program could throw at them. There is no need to structure calculus along the lines of the AP program owing to the fact that the students may already be well beyond the expectations of the AP program and involved with work that they are more likely to see in the second or third year of their college education.

In an event that I suppose is rarely ever seen now, I watched a classmate in the 1970's gain admission to Harvard after his junior year with no high school diploma in hand. His incredibly facile brain had already made high school work unnecessary, and Harvard was more than happy to take him into the fold. Lesser academicians marveled at this young man and reveled in his good fortune. If he could get into Harvard then surely another year in our school would serve each of us well.

Although Advanced Placement exams were in place then, for the most part we ignored them, secure in the knowledge that our years in school were not something for us to fritter away. Remarkably, this young man simply took challenging courses taught by demanding teachers who gave their time and expertise freely. Had a certain teacher not taken his time to introduce me to the works of Samuel Beckett, my own love for the avant-garde theater might never have grown the way it did. Honors courses are not everything.

Teachers who teach students as if they were teaching their own peers are those who make the difference. These teachers fully understand that they are educating young people, but expect them to weave words and solve problems with the skill of an adult. Such expectations help students rise to the occasion, and lead them forward in ways that AP courses do not.

At one day school, a teacher was renowned for educating students who seldom failed to receive 4's or 5's on their AP exams. Unfortunately, although these courses had the honors and AP labels attached to them, the students were not educated in the fine art of Calculus. Rather, they were taught to take a test. In college, the demands are different, and I sometimes wonder how these students, taught to take a specific test, fared when college instructors demanded that they do more than solve a problem that they had already seen in a hundred different ways.

At the other end of the spectrum, the size of the small boarding schools does not allow for the specialization that can result at a large elite school. The assumption that a superior student will not get an excellent preparatory education under such circumstances is foolish. Certainly, at less selective schools, students are not likely to be challenged as much as they might at an elite school. However, those superior students fill a special niche in such schools.

When educators at run across a jewel, they go out of their way to educate that student to the best of their ability. Each year, a number of the students from less influential schools are offered admission to elite universities while the other end of the academic spectrum is challenged to find any school that will accept them. One student will go to Brown, and another in the same classroom will attend a school whose selectivity is only defined by a basic pulse check at interview time. How can this be?

The answer is a reason that may cause you take a good look at a lesser-known school. At a large elite school, your brilliant children will shine, but they will shine in the company of another few hundred brilliant children. Within that massive glow, any child can get lost. Not so at a school that struggles to make its academic name. Superior students rise to the top of the class. They win academic awards, merit scholarships, and approbation within the school, and the respect of their fellow students. As a result, their academic confidence soars, as do their chances of admission to elite universities.

For many students then, attendance at a seemingly inferior school can be a great plus. The old adage about big fish in small ponds holds true to this day. If your child can shine in a small, comfortable, less academically pressured environment, they will be able to gain more than you can imagine. Each year, the Ivy League schools admit more than their share of students who are not the product of AP pushing, honors rushing schools. Schools of strength

71

attract and seek out students whose personal characteristics stand out. So long as the environment of the third tier school is healthy, it might be the perfect choice for your child.

Boarding schools throw a seductive number your way in every piece of information they send to you. Classes, they assure you, are small in size- small enough to make sure that your child will not be lost in a crowd. Don't believe it until you see it in practice. There are two statistics that come into play. The faculty to student ratio is arrived at simply enough. Schools take the number of teachers, divide them by the number of students enrolled, and behold, you have a student to teacher ratio of one to six. Such numbers can be deceptive.

That small ratio is most helpful when student and teacher share the same space. If the teacher is seldom seen after the school day, then the ratio begins to rise. A better question to ask of the school is what the ratio of student to faculty is in the dormitories or immediate campus. Six to one is wonderful when the school demands that its teachers maintain a presence on campus, and in your child's life, for an amount of time that makes the ratio meaningful.

Classes at boarding school, almost invariably, are smaller than the average public school class, insuring a more personalized education. Some schools though will be less than faithful in their adherence to small class sizes, and fall in the middle range between independent and public schools. When money is tight, class sizes rise accordingly. As such, one of the great advantages of boarding schools is diluted when finances dictate class size.

Either during the tour of the school, or during a subsequent visit to classes for your child, (Always recommended — only in that way will a student truly understand whether or not they actually belong in a given community) keep sticking your nose into the classroom. If the school's class size ratios say ten to one, and many classes seem to have over twenty, you know everything you need to know.
Wouldn't you rather that a school was honest in its estimate of class size?

The smaller numbers always sound better, but larger classes aren't awful. A ratio of sixteen to one is actually still within the acceptable range for class size. From that point forward however, teachers are unable to pay adequate attention to all of the students in the class, and your child is that much more likely to receive less than what the school promises. This problem is most likely in evidence at schools where financial realities dictate that classes be a certain size before the school can authorize hiring a teacher.

Imagine this scenario: A school is watching its classics program shrinks in size, with class sizes dipping under ten students on a regular basis. In that situation, Latin and Greek become less and less feasible in a school that does not possess a large endowment. Soon, the school is forced to make a decision. Do they keep the Classics program alive for the sake of academic purity, or let the course lapse for financial security? Any school still teaching the Classics these days has made a choice that small classes are justified when academic legitimacy is at stake.

Always look at a school's low number programs- Art, Music, Theater, Latin, Greek, Photography, and see if they are kept alive with low numbers. If they are, the school is at least passing honest when they say that small class size is something the hold dear. If those classes aren't there, and you see big classes on your walk-through, you are being misled. Worst of all, the school fully understands that it is misleading you. Ask yourself a simple question then and there- is the place you want your child to call second home for the next four years?

Does "lights out" at your school really mean lights out? What <u>really</u> happens...?

After the bad experience of my sophomore year roommate, I committed to getting a single the following years. It was a mixed blessing; I had my own space, but no other in the room to discourage the "fun" that classmates could have.

Many times at around 3:00am, there would be a SLAM as my door was burst open, bright light as the switch was hit, and three or four guys in trench coats and Halloween masks screaming in my just awakened face. They had been partying or were just bored. It happened often enough that I actually became blasé about it.

"Just turn off the lights." I would say as I rolled over towards the wall. After a while, the worst they could do was leaving the lights on, forcing me to get up and turn them off. These attacks stopped toward the end of my junior year, since they could not get a rise out of me anymore. S.P.

So what really goes on at boarding school after the lights go out? There's no way to list all the behaviors, so I won't try. However, the culture that develops after the clock strikes midnight is anything but healthy. What's more, it's nearly impossible to determine exactly what goes on at a given school. Therefore, I'll treat it all as a "worst case scenario", realizing that some elements are true to some schools and others true to a different set.

The best "worst case scenario" involves academic work. Teachers have certainly not become less demanding over the years, and if anything, they have given more and more homework to kids as time has passed. The resulting situation is that students at boarding schools are flat overloaded with work. The teachers will deny it up and down, but there is no escaping this fact.

In some schools, a given course's work literally takes over the culture of the school for up to a week. During that period, all other work becomes secondary to the major project or paper due at the end of the week. Instead of getting a good night's rest, students become completely involved with the paper to the negligence of all else. So, a kid's work suffers while she struggles to make do. Math assignments go undone, books aren't read for English, and a student gets behind, destined to never catch up until the end of the term and a lengthy vacation.

74

Don't be surprised when your child comes home from boarding school and sleeps for three days. It's part of the routine. The most disturbing aspect of this routine is the institutional acceptance. For reasons unknown, schools will accept this ritual as part of the canonical law of the institution. That's not to say that the teachers won't complain. They will, loudly, to both student and teacher. In the end though, the ritual continues unabated, despite the fact that schools know that studying after midnight doesn't help a student perform effectively. In point of fact, studying after midnight produces diminishing returns, no matter what your child tells you. Be wary then of schools that seem to have rights of passage that revolve around late night work and "all-nighters." While these experiences are fun for kids, they are not helpful in any way.

The other after-midnight activities are more disturbing. As a rule, schools do not have a great deal of staff coverage after midnight. Hence, all bets are off when it comes to supervision for your child. Schools that take the night hours seriously actually make an effort to cover from midnight to six AM. However, that's the impossible dream. For each child that a late night crew can get to bed, there's another that is up doing God knows what. No matter how hard a school tries, they can't account for all of the kids. Important then is the manner in which the school deals with the whole child.

Dorm personnel, Deans of Students, faculty, and administration must all be involved in a concerted effort to make sure that students understand that when the hands on the clock move past midnight, the preferred activity is sleep. What's more, if a student cannot sleep eight hours AND get their academic work done, the problem is the school's, not the child's. If that happens, then the school must look hard at the student's situation, and put measures into place that prepare the student for a successful academic career. That's when the kids start to see midnight as a time to sleep.

The after midnight culture is deeply troubling. If there is any element of society that is singly destructive to children, it is the culture that supports the use of drugs and alcohol. No school supports drug and alcohol use. Some though go to greater lengths

75

to ensure that the community is healthy. How?

Again, you need to look to the schools structure for the support systems that are needed. First, make sure that schools make a concerted effort to educate their students about drugs and alcohol. Freedom from Chemical Dependency is one of the most widely recognized organizations, and schools that bring such groups in show that they are serious. Why? The kind of education that is delivered by a recognized substance abuse group doesn't come cheap. That doesn't stop schools who put the children first. Even schools with limited financial resources will spend the money to educate their children in ways that they cannot.

Be wary of schools that don't put money into education that will teach students how to succeed in the craft of life. Your child will be more likely to get their education about drugs and alcohol from fellow students. That's not where you want your kids to learn lessons that will last a long time.

For as long as pot has been available in boarding schools, it has been there. Sometimes a dry spell hits, but mostly, the dope is present and available. It's merely logical when you think about it. The more wealthy elements of society have always had ready access to illicit materials, and pot is no different. In addition, the thirty some years that pot has been a part of the mainstream American culture has had a curious effect on kids. While this is not true of all, a solid percentage of kids don't see pot as a troublesome drug. In addition, because the drug is illicit, dope is more readily obtainable than alcohol. Alcohol is purchased through legitimate outlets. Pot comes through different channels- channels that students can easily discover.

I've seen marijuana come in the mail, in care packages from home, bought on trips to concerts, and delivered by school employees. No school is safe from marijuana. Unfortunately, that doesn't scare too many people anymore. It should. There is certainly ample evidence that adolescent use of the drug is extremely harmful to a child. The children of boarding schools though, self-educated on the dangers of drugs, don't often believe the rhetoric thrust toward them by

76

schools (or sadly, the hired guns of the trade). And so they will keep on toking, whether they are gifted or intellectually challenged. They simply aren't aware of the dangers involved.

Schools frequently respond by putting serious consequences in place for drug use. The punishments for use of marijuana range from instant expulsion to minimal suspension or even in-house penalties. Surprisingly, in the marijuana culture, kids press on regardless of the penalties. The use of the drug becomes a game that they play with the faculty- can they, bright kids, get away with it?

Truth be told, they can. The tools they use for smoking are remarkable, culled from the science lab, the shop, or even the fruit basket at dinner. One of the more recent developments is the "Bounty" tube. Made from a few sheets of laundry softener and a toilet paper tube, kids can take a hit from a pipe and blow the smoke out through the tube. The odor is covered by the Bounty, and the faculty none the wiser.

Within the culture, the more that a student gets away with, the more a student believes that they can do. Unfortunately, despite protestations that marijuana is not a gateway drug, in a boarding school environment, it is just that. Schools that don't make a serious effort to put the clamps on marijuana use are buying themselves, and more importantly their students, a whole mess of trouble.

Kids will swear up and down that pot doesn't lead to more serious drug use. In a perfect world, it doesn't. For kids prone to substance abuse however, pot will be their gateway drug. And in boarding schools, more than pot will be available. Over a twenty five year period, I've seen or heard of LSD, Ecstasy, speed, cocaine, morphine, opium, hashish, even heroin. The less restrictive atmosphere of boarding school (i.e. no one always looking over the shoulder) allows these drugs to make it to campus somehow, and into the hands of the kids.

Yes, it could happen at home too, but the boarding school environment makes it easier. Not that your child will automatically become involved, but the presence of the drugs themselves is actually dangerous whether or not your child takes them. In many schools, being in the presence of kids breaking rules, even if you are not breaking the rule yourself, are grounds for suspension or dismissal. Moreover, kids won't think twice about the safety of anyone other than themselves. When your child is sitting in the room, the only reason they'll be asked to leave is if the other student perceives that she is in danger of being caught BECAUSE your child is there.

Perception rules the day in boarding schools. If a kid is perceived as a narc no one is going to break a rule when they believe the other child is going to turn them in to the authorities. Even in that there is good and bad. Kids in need of friends can be ostracized as narcs. Their only choices are to sit in loneliness or make a bad choice. Too many young people served well by boarding school have had their careers cut short by rules there to protect them. Unfortunate then, is the fact that the rules don't protect the kids from themselves.

Do not count on boarding schools to remove drugs and the temptation to use them from the life of your child. If anything, they will make it more possible than it was before. Hence, if you are sending your child into a boarding school environment, do not stop talking about drugs with them. If anything, embrace the conversation more. Your child still needs the parental contact.

What if something goes wrong at school?

There were no professional counselors at the school I attended. At least, I was ignorant of any. What we had was the rector who taught Old and New Testament classes and, of course, was in charge of Thursday and Sunday chapel. He was very approachable, as I knew since he was also my adviser, but with 400 or so students, he could not advise them all. At least he, and others on the faculty were approachable, but the lack of someone who is trained and committed to adolescent issues can have serious repercussions.

During my years there, I never heard of any actual suicide attempts at school (although I was out at the edge of the social information loop). Of the few kids who were in the "planning" stage I did hear about, it was handled internally by upperclassmen, once by buying the kid a Coke and telling him to relax. It helped, but it was hardly professional help. The culture of the school was such that personal problems of all sorts were not to be reported to the faculty or staff until it had escalated to the point they would have noticed anyway.

A child in crisis is the single most troubling part of the culture of a boarding school, as their actions, emotions and decisions have the most substantial effect on the life a school. With a child in crisis, anything can, and will happen. Particularly because schools work to ensure that crisis won't occur, they are often ill prepared when they do. I have known far too many teachers that have had to perform "above and beyond the call of duty." The fact that these teachers exist is praiseworthy. In fact, if you take a good look at the faculty at a boarding school, you will see, in spite of their own oddities, a group that includes more than its fair share of well-minded, committed individuals.

Whether that is enough to help when the moment of crisis occurs isn't even a question for debate. Nothing can prepare a school for that moment. The only manner of control that a school has in a crisis moment is their actions before the crisis. Crises-es don't come from out of the blue, even though they might seem to. To a trained eye, the signs of crisis are evident before a kid suddenly crashes and burns.

Allow me to reiterate that counseling programs at schools are incredibly important components of the residential life aspect of a boarding school. Do not think that your child is immune from the dangers caused by crisis. If your child is well adjusted and quite able to deal with the pressures of boarding school life, you might assume she would be fine. Unfortunately, as observed before, boarding schools are not places where children live in a vacuum. Their lives are affected by the actions of other children, sometimes to the point where a child in crisis makes a new crisis.

Imagine a child (particularly a younger child) rooming with an older, at-risk child. You might initially believe that the older child will be a stable force in your child's life, and the school could labor under that belief as well. Watch out when the crisis hits. The worst case I've heard is that of a child that made a suicide attempt, and then was returned to live with the same, much younger roommate. This was a horrible scenario for all involved.

The younger roommate was understandably terrified, with the older still only a week or so removed from crisis. Some schools would behave as if the attempt had never happened in the first place. Indeed, what can they do? No one will likely accept a roommate change, and you don't want to place the crisis child alone in a room. Add to all of this the fact that it's difficult for a school to release a child for psychiatric reasons. Actually, allow me to amend that. Few schools can afford to release children for psychiatric reasons alone. The need to fill beds at schools make them businesses that will try to determine exactly how far they can go before a child can no longer function on campus. In many cases, the measure of that determination is whether or not the crisis child represents a danger to other children on campus.

Wrangle with that for a moment. How can you determine exactly when the child becomes a danger? Realistically, at any given time, a substantive number of students are moving around crisis- they simply are not all identified. This is where your view of the school, and awareness of all its support programs, is in high demand. Conservatively, a school should have at least one full time, trained psychological counselor on staff. Naturally, this is a position where schools wrestle with the dynamics of dollars and cents. Counselors aren't always the busiest people on campus, and their lack of business can trouble a school's business manager. No matter how you look at it, the presence of a counselor demands that a school raise tuition to cover the cost. When you consider that compensation packages for faculty run higher than tuition allows, suddenly the cost of a counselor adds another hefty chunk to the tuition for everyone in a 200-child school. Parents don't like those numbers much.

How would you react though, if a school told you, quite honestly, that the rise in tuition was there specifically to cover the cost of bringing a full-time counselor? Hopefully, you understand that the need for a counselor is essential. After the cost of a counselor, schools need to look at other members of a counseling staff as well. If you've ever been in counseling, you understand that one counselor is not sufficient for all. If a school is large, employing more counselors is an extremely wise move.

At least one school has taken this step further, employing dorm personnel whose backgrounds are in counseling, not teaching. During the day, they are not responsible for classes, but their evenings come to life as they are asked to cover the dorm not just as a place to study, but also as a place for children to experience the full spectrum of their life. Trained, prepared and focused dorm counselors can avert crisis. The triple threat may still be the rule in boarding schools, but I'm certain that a number of teachers who have left boarding schools will tell you that they are better teachers and coaches when they are not focused on trying to counsel kids in a dorm structure as well.

If a school doesn't have trained dorm counselors, they should have a working relationship with a local counseling group. Once again though, the nature of boarding schools makes that a problem. Most small schools are still rural, and counseling offices aren't usually right at hand. Therefore, the counseling needs of students are filled either by bringing in counselors, or by sending students off to counseling sessions off campus. Once again, these are imperfect solutions at best.

The best a school can offer is only possible at large, well-funded schools. Such schools are able to offer a full-time counseling program with a number of counselors. In practice, these programs are enormously successful. They provide anonymity for the students, full-time access to a counselor (which is exactly what a child in crisis needs) and professional assessment of the dangers to the student and her peers.

Talk at length with a school about how it handles counseling issues, even if your child seems okay. They should be able to present you with a well-coordinated and implemented plan for kids in crisis, and for how they meet the daily needs of children. If you listen to an admissions representative hem and haw about the topic, you are correct in your concern about just what life at the school will be like for the students.

Be careful of schools who think that they can do the counseling themselves. They can't, and the result of their hubris might be a disaster. Too many times, students don't return home from boarding school. Don't send your child to a school whose program indicates they are trying to replace the professionals with the belief that they are good enough to handle anything. They aren't, and you'll see the difference in how the school runs.

How strict is the school's disciplinary policy?

On the December night of a senior's birthday, he and two junior friends snuck into a teacher's home and stole the keys to the senior's car. They obtained a fair amount of liquor and went out on the town, ending with their arrest while drunkenly stealing street signs. The first call woke up the Dean at 4am, telling him that the police had three of his students in custody and could he please come get them. The second call you never want to get or make was the 6am call to the three families to come and get their children that day and take them home. This is why my graduating class had 98, not 100 students the next year. The question is, why did the students think that this wouldn't be the result? S.P.

There are a lot of phone calls that parents look forward to receiving. Advisers will call with good news about grades. Kids will call to tell you that they had a great day in the game. Sometimes, they'll even call just to hear the sound of your voice. A lot of kids make calls from boarding school each year that are not quite so welcome. Faculty members make them too. If your luck is bad, you might make the call yourself. I know I said no anecdotes, but this one is worth telling.

One fine evening, I chewed out all the boys in my dorm about their slovenly behavior. Their rooms were a mess, the trustees were on their way, parent's weekend was two days away, and they were just being adolescent boys. In a fury, I told them that if they didn't clean their rooms, I was going to clean them myself. The next morning, most had cleaned their rooms, but two, both advisees of mine, had decided not to heed my warning. With first period free, I entered their room to clean. Within about two minutes of cleaning, I discovered the cardboard containers from about four cases of beers neatly folded (yes, I see the irony- they didn't) beneath a desk. Next, I turned to their refrigerator, where I found what I didn't want to find. Two six packs of beer.

Obviously, the next step was to call the Dean of Students and get the wheels of the discipline system in action. I returned to my study to do just that, when suddenly, the phone rang. John's father. Of course. He wanted to know what to bring John for the weekend. My answer was simple enough- "Come early, and only stay for a little time—you need to take John home with you." I stifled a laugh, and then went off and took care of the rest of the tasks.

If you are like most parents, you'll never have to work with the discipline structure of the school. The vast majority of students don't get in big trouble. Those that do though are right in the middle of one a school's most important structures. The effectiveness of a school's discipline system plays a direct role in the effectiveness of the school as a whole. There are as many discipline programs as schools, and their sole goal is to somehow maintain order in a situation that can easily descend into chaos. If the students respect the discipline system, then chances are that the school will function effectively.

That is not to say that students will not break school rules. That is going to happen whether schools like it or not. An effective discipline system will however control the actions of the students to a great degree. Discipline problems run the gamut from missing class to serious drug and alcohol violations, even theft and assault. How a school metes out punishment dictates how the students will respond. You can easily find the rules of a school in the books, along with the punishments. Rarely will this system appear anything less than completely fair. The major problem is that discipline systems are defined and implemented by individuals. If those individuals are viewed as too lax, the students will walk all over them. If they are viewed as stern to an excess degree, student morale will reflect their actions.

The Dean of Students is a difficult job, and it must be filled by an individual capable of walking the fine line between leniency and strident application of discipline. In addition, that Dean must also be able to harness the goodwill of the faculty, and instill in students a sense of trust and goodwill. The finest deans are those that students love in spite of their role as the master of discipline. During your interview, try and find a moment with Dean of Students to talk about the discipline system. If they have the time, you already know that for at least that day, they are not chasing down a discipline case. You'll also be able to tell from speaking with that person if they espouse a form of discipline that is in keeping with your own ethos. They will explain the system clearly—more clearly than the view book can. If you don't like what you hear, you know what to do.

You will discover that alcohol violations and drug violations are dealt with in different ways. Some schools use a two-week suspension as a major deterrent. Having never experienced a suspension first hand, I am forced to go to the testimony of a former boarding school classmate. Those two weeks, he said, were essential parts of his growth.

Left at home with little to do, he was forced to take a hard look at himself. He understood that he was privileged, but felt, like so many adolescents, bulletproof. His suspension served to redirect his energies in a positive direction. That redirection colored his life, and his leadership in the future. Other classmates took those two weeks to study hard for the first time. Less strenuous schools may stress that taking a child out of class for two weeks will cause irreparable harm. They are gravely mistaken.

Short (3-5 day) suspensions serve more as vacations than punishments. Students don't get drastically behind, and they get the message that the school just doesn't believe that a severe punishment is justified. The same schools are also the ones that will turn around and expel a student after the light suspension. Two weeks gets their attention, and yours. Look for such strength in a boarding school.

Look also for how they deal with students returning from suspension. This is a question that you cannot ask during an interview- your child is likely to be in attendance at a boarding school when you have the chance to address the issue. If a suspension has the proper effect on a child, she will be chastened. More than a few former classmates have told me that their two-week suspension from school was one of the most important events in their life.

Without question, a lengthy suspension will have an enormous effect on a child's life, particularly if the parents do all they can to insure that the time spent at home isn't akin to a vacation. When a student realizes that her behavior has bought her nothing except hard work and academic deficiency, she may well think twice when faced with a bad choice again. How the school deals with the returning child is equally important.

On one hand, some schools tell their faculty to treat the child as if nothing had happened (as if that were possible) and do everything they can to help the child come joyfully back into the community. This sends an awful message to the child. The school is saying, in essence, that the infraction was something that happened and should be forgotten by all involved. Nothing could be more destructive for the child and the discipline process.

Children actually want adults to care about what they did, and expect that we will be aware of what they did wrong. Adolescents, so focused on what the world thinks of them, need to be supported in that thought. If we ignore the infraction, then the student gets a message that says the problem was getting caught, not the actual infraction.

One effective way that schools deal with these students is by placing them on supervised probation, where they have a probation counselor (usually a teacher) who directs their time after a suspension. Naturally, not all students respond to this action well, but it is a far sight better than allowing the student to run free after a suspension. A suspension is the worst a school can do to a child short of expulsion, and the student needs to understand clearly that their actions must change.

Probation counselors can meet with students regularly and explain the "why" of the punishment, and offer guidance as to how the student can avoid making the same mistake again. In addition, that counselor is also able to get a solid look at how the child exists within the school culture, thereby giving the probation counselor a clearer view of the school culture. Truly, this is a win-win situation for all involved. A child might feel as if the school is overly aware of the infraction, but that is far superior to the student shrinking back into the shadows of school's subculture, taking chances with the risk of expulsion.

Another facet of the school's discipline system that you must consider is the very ethos of the system itself. Boarding schools make their policies in a manner that ideally represents a codified set of rules that aid the school in pursuing its mission with students. The rules are designed to redirect students who do not thrive in the mission, or do not grow to reflect the mission of the school lived out in them. Logically then, you must have a concrete understanding of the school's rule structure before you commit a child to its custody. Otherwise, you will end up with a child punished for things that make no sense to you, and other students not punished for things that do.

Somewhere there is a school that still allows tobacco use among its students despite all of the state laws that forbid the use of tobacco. If you run across a school that allows such use, and you do not condone the use of tobacco products by your child, you are well within your rights to ask the school about that tobacco policy. Why do they allow it? Why is there a smoker's area? The answer will have to do with the mission and culture of the institution.

The school may believe that their time is better spent trying to ward off other behaviors, or consider tobacco use the least of their worries. In their circumstances, those facts could be reasonable, but you've got to wonder if that's the right place for your child. While examining the ethos, look also at what they consider major violations, and how they punish the child in the circumstances. In some cases, you will find schools that consider pot smoking and skipping class in the same light, administering the same punishment for very different acts.

If you cannot understand why this is true before you send your child to that school, you will be less understanding when your child is suddenly suffering the maximum penalty for breaking a rule that you believe is petty. Having had more than one conversation with a parent about just this type of offense, I can assure you that you will not be at your most rational when discussing the issue. Check particularly what constitutes grounds for immediate expulsion.

I know schools where lighting a match in a building elicits immediate expulsion, no questions asked, while drinking a six pack in your room brought out the standard two-week suspension. On this surface this rule seems to be complete overkill. If you dig a bit deeper, you'll find that the school once had a dorm fire. A no fatality dorm fire, but a dorm fire nonetheless. Therefore, fire was banned from within the buildings. No one wanted to see a repeat of that incident.

When students were expelled for breaking this rule, other schools welcomed them in, marveling at the severity of the policy. As a parent, you have to buy into the rules of the school, whether you love all of them or not. First off, there is no way that you are ever going to get a rule changed or altered for your child's case. Schools should not do it. Read the handbook carefully, and check for all the things the rules cover and don't. If you send your child to that school, spend precious time talking about the rules of the school and what they represent to your child. If your child is in the position of attending an elite school, the last thing that you, or them, want is for that career to be cut short by the discipline system.

For financial aid students, this is an even greater concern. I stayed straight for nearly four years because of the threat of removal of my scholarship. While schools usually offer need-based financial aid, they also have the right to change those financial aid packages. Your child needs to remember that if he wants to play with the rule structure. Once a child is fired from an elite boarding school, they cannot simply reapply to another. The financial aid is not waiting to be tapped. Those empty beds are there for full-pay students who will help pay the bills.

This discussion is severe, but the school rules are the rhetoric (aside from the academic regimen) that decides whether or not your child can stay at a school. No matter what, make sure that your child does not hand the power of his future to the school. The rules will guide him effectively toward success, so long as they represent a logical set of beliefs in concert with yours. If not, do not make life for the school hard, and your own miserable, be placing with a child in a school that you do not believe in.

Do boarding schools have a problem with drug and alcohol abuse?

Unless you are keenly aware of social changes, you've got no idea of what is going on in the drug and alcohol culture of the school. Some of the faculty have an understanding, but the kids at schools are far more likely to have them beat at every corner. For years, I was proud of the record of my students when it came to drug and alcohol offenses. Naively, I assumed that my good work had earned their respect, and led them to obey the rules.

Right.

The boys in my house had a habit of coming to me right abound lights out time asking to take a shower. Having no problems with cleanliness, and trusting my senior boys (first mistake) I always acceded. To the showers they went, and the beers were passed under the shower stall wall. I was never the wiser.

Though they usually carry similar penalties, the use of alcohol versus the use of marijuana places it in a different category altogether. Where do they part ways? While it is illegal for a child to consume alcoholic beverages at school, we live in a society where the consumption of alcohol is legal for anyone over the age of twenty-one. In many families, alcohol consumption is an accepted part of that culture. As a result, boarding schools have a unique alcohol culture with a variety of facets and problems.

Let's take them on one at a time. Faculty members don't make it easy. I've yet to find a boarding school where alcohol doesn't flow rather freely in faculty circles. The year opens with alcohol driven parties, faculties celebrate with alcohol at Christmas, and knock back cold beers when the kids take off for vacation. As a former boarding school teacher, I'll make no value judgments about those acts because I was there with a beer in hand like the rest. End of the year parties aren't the problem though. Middle of the year parties are.

Young faculty members are central to boarding schools. These teachers are essential to boarding schools. They are cheap, tireless, playful, and thoroughly involved with the students. That's where the problems begin. More than a few boarding school stories are peppered with tales of teachers and students drinking together. At one time, it represented a virtual rite of passage at schools. Today, fewer teachers make such errors, due in no small part to the effective work of master teachers and deans doing student affairs work.

Unfortunately, this doesn't stop teachers from making mistakes that the kids won't let anyone know about. It's hard to find a town in America that doesn't have a bar somewhere close. Young faculty will find that bar, and they will drink. As a result, they will also model behaviors for kids that are completely unacceptable.

Young teachers still stumble onto the hall after a long night at the local pub. They still drive when they shouldn't. And kids, still awake (as we discussed earlier) still see these behaviors. What's the effect? When teachers are predictable in their actions, kids will be the same. The best time — the BEST time to party is in the window when your dorm counselor is out tying one on. When they return, it's still a good time, because the counselors know that the last thing they should do is step out onto the hall to check on how things are going. A drunken teacher will head to his apartment, close the door, turn on the TV, and pray that students don't knock on the door.

Again, this is not a value judgment, but simply the truth. The teacher is actually doing the right thing by hiding away. In this case though, doing the right thing is also synonymous with doing the wrong thing. How many of you expect that your child's counselor will be unprepared at the time when the counselor is necessary?

Boarding schools make an implicit promise that faculty are there 24/7 to take care of you children. The truth is that for as much as they are there, there is also a time when a percentage of teachers won't be ready. God forbid that time is the time when your child needs an adult badly. A teacher whose judgment is impaired by alcohol is not the person you need. Boarding schools will tell you this is a rare occurrence, and in fairness, it probably is rare.

The next side of the question centers on the actions of older teachers. If society has its fair share of alcoholics, so do boarding schools. Some thankfully are in recovery and able to effectively discharge their duties. Others though are still caught in the web. In a conventional world, alcoholism is a terrifying disease that tears families and lives apart. In a boarding school world, the effect is far more pronounced effecting students and faculty alike. Students are forced to witness the slow (or rapid) disintegration of an individual they trusted to guide their lives. In the worst cases, faculty suddenly act in a manner that forces them to leave the boarding community. Boarding communities don't deal with sudden change well, and the sudden loss of a teacher has a resounding effect.

Alcoholism isn't the sole territory of teachers either. Many, many children taste their first alcohol in boarding school when they might not have experienced it until later in life. Others find the taste so appealing that they begin the process of making the possession of alcohol a full time job. Any individual who is serious about drinking can get alcohol, and the best can also hide it with remarkable effectiveness. Before you know it, those students are fully involved in drinking on a daily basis, sacrificing work and sleep, just like the students involved with drugs. They do however have one major advantage in feeding their addiction. While schools can be extremely proactive in dealing with drug use by putting in place screening and education programs, you can't catch a kid drinking three days later. The result is that the young alcoholic is living in the perfect atmosphere to feed the habit. Only when the students become more and more brazen in their actions do they finally get noticed. By that point, for many, it is far too late. If they have developed a dependency there is a major problem. How do schools deal with these casualties of alcohol? Thankfully, some schools have both counseling programs and the wisdom to place kids with Alcoholics Anonymous.

However, the very fact that I'm telling you this shows the failure of the schools to provide anonymity for children struggling with major issues. AA is supposed to be anonymous, but if you travel to a school campus, you'll find out exactly who attends their weekly meetings- and who doesn't. Kids know who the drinkers are, and which ones are serious about recovery. What's the worst of this? Imagine sending your child to a school for the academics and family atmosphere, only to discover that a number of kids there are actually trying to climb back into a world that was shattered by drugs and alcohol.

There is no practical way that an adolescent can be expected to handle the paradoxes inherent in such situations, and schools do not prepare them for to wrestle with paradox. Child after child is then expected to live with, and counsel, kids who are either in crisis or at risk. Kids can't help kids with alcohol problems, and they can't help kids with drug problems. Their social order demands that they try to help, and also demands that they do not let any adult know what's happening. I thought that I was gifted to identify kids at risk, but found out the hard way that no matter how much I thought I was on the inside, I was always standing outside looking in. As a faculty member I could help, but the secret world of substance abuse remained. Some secrets you don't let anyone see.

Why is the interview so important?

I always wondered at the admissions office keeping yearbooks lying around in the office. What would a parent make of a picture of a heavyset junior with a bovine expression assumed for the camera with the caption from Animal House; "Fat, drunk, and stupid is no way to go through life."? S.P.

The formal interview is for the school. In this interview visit, they will tour the school with you, give you background on the school's history, feed answers to questions, and generally let you know who THEY believe they are.

Your responsibility is to discern whether or not the school is actually being honest to what it presents and prctices.

In an interview situation, you are destined to see a school on its best behavior. Listen closely to what the tour guide says as she leads you around the school. Does the guide seem down to earth and honest about the school, or do they seem to be reciting a prepared script? A tour guide can tell you a great deal.

Naturally, tour guides are the school's best kids. They are freshly scrubbed, prepared with answers and excited to host your visit. Ask them questions. If they seem ill at ease with questions about their school, they may well be in a situation where they feel that they can comfortably tell you the truth.

Look at what parts of the school they show you. Unquestionably, the dorm rooms you will see reflect the nicest accommodations on campus, and belong to the neatest kids. In most cases, schools have rooms prepared for showing- no school is going to show you its worst rooms. That therefore, is probably a great question to ask. "Are all the dorm rooms as nice as this one?" Watch for a reaction. If the rooms in the house across campus are not suitable, you will see it in their eyes.

Examine the walls hard with your eyes. I doubt that this event has recurred, but for entertainment's sake:

At the opening of a school year, I was giving my dorm the last walk through before I anticipated the arrival of students and parents. I popped down to one last room, the proctor's, and heard a strange scratching noise. I took a good look at the wall and noticed it was, well, moving. Throwing caution to the wind I pulled down the wallpaper to reveal thousands of thoroughly involved cockroaches. Needless to say, the first call was to physical plant, and eliminating cockroaches became job one.

So look at the walls of the dorm - even look around a bit for graffiti if you can. Go to the extreme and stop by the bathroom to take a look. Bathrooms will tell you a lot about a school. If a dorm bathroom is littered with derogatory remarks about the headmaster, you can go back to the admissions director armed with questions as to why there are those kinds of things written on the walls. As they are the marketers, they'll want to know what you saw. Take a good look at the classrooms too. Don't just look at a desk, try one out and see how it might feel to be in a class at the school.

The legendary Harkness (big, oval, for about sixteen kids and a teacher) table gives a classroom a unique feel. In addition, that table guarantees that class size will remain small. They don't make Harkness tables for twenty students, so those tables are evidence of a certain kind of teaching: teaching that involves the art of direct contact and query with students. At a Harkness table, you cannot slip into the background. Look for them.

Stop by the dining hall too. Three times every day, your child is going to sit down here for a meal. It doesn't take a trained eye to see whether the food is any good or not. In addition, if you take a good look at the kid's trays, you'll see if they've got good eating on their mind, or a sincere desire to eat as much Captain Crunch and drink as much chocolate milk as humanly possible. You will find some real gems out there too. Putney School is notorious for hot rolls during morning break, and phenomenal homemade meals for all other times. A visit is worth the time if only for the food.

Take a look at the computer lab, and computer policies you see posted as well. Substantial numbers of boarding schools require laptop computers for all of their students, yet some do not. What's the difference between these schools? First, any school that has to rely upon technology in order to justify its academic programs is reaching for a solution. Technology must exist in schools, and the common standard these days seems to be universal connectivity for students. Some schools still hold out though, and they are well worth a look.

Talk with the admissions officer about technology, and what the school's planned uses for technology are. That's the important question. Schools can have remarkable technology structure in place, but without a concrete sense of how they are going to use that technology, the infrastructure is useless. There's only so much you can pick up in such a visit, and you certainly do risk taking too much time from a busy day.

Advise your child to behave truthfully in the interview. School admissions personnel work extremely hard to put together a group of students that adequately reflects, or should gain from involvement with, the mission of the school. Make sure that your child dresses in a manner appropriate to the school, and emphasize that they need to respond with truthful statements. If they do, chances are more likely that their personality will shine through, and the admissions committee will be well prepared to make a decision that is best for all parties. The worst thing an admissions staff can do is pick the wrong child for the mission. Do not make yourself over to be attractive to a school. If you are the right family, you, and they, will most certainly know.

Finally, is boarding school a good or bad thing?

Most of my memories about boarding school are, frankly, negative. I was the small kid at the bottom of the social strata in a land of unlocked doors, after all. But I am just one person with one person's experiences. I have good memories, too.

Trying to explain to the dorm master why the hallways were an inch deep in water and all the fire-extinguishers empty after an epic water fight between me and five dorm mates (for the record? I more than held my own, wet as I ended up). Hours long rounds of hearts in my room with the good friends I did make, many of whom I am still in contact with. The camaraderie of the swim team; I have a very vivid (and cherished) memory of pulling down my lane and seeing team mates shouting encouragement from the pool side, pushing me to push harder. Absorbing academic information and learning how to process it is one of the best things I got out of a low-distraction environment. Friday night Miami Vice in the TV room, where we all had the show in common.

Good times. Not always, but it will be the same at any high-school. Boarding school just kicks up the intensity a bit. S.P.

Many boarding schools are extremely fond of calling themselves a family. In the wake of <u>Casualties of Privilege</u> and <u>Healthy Choices, Healthy Schools</u>, many schools went so far as to change the name of their dorm master, or dorm counselors, to dorm parents. The schools emphasize the family lifestyle, make dorm units smaller, and generally try to present a face to the world that says "family."

Would that it were so.

However much a school wants to be thought of as a family, the truth is that they never become that for a child. When a student leaves a school, they carry with them fond memories, but they are seldom possessed of the emotional ties that bring them to the school to visit year after year. They may for a while after graduation, but in time, the new students in the community change the nature of what a school calls a "family."

So what are we left with? In reading this book, you may have come to the opinion that I have an ax to grind with the boarding school world. Nothing could be further from the truth. I visit St. Mark's when I can, cheer the teams, and walk in timeworn spots. Given the chance to live my life over again, boarding school would still be a part of the picture. However problematic my tenure was, it was the defining experience of my life. I was privileged to learn from masters of their discipline, share athletic exploits with my fellow students, laugh in the wee hours of the morning, and play a game called cloister-ball until I was driven to distraction. I also must confess that I still have more than a bit of jealousy every time I hear a child say that they are headed for boarding school. I know they are about to embark upon a special journey.

Obviously then, I'm the last person that will tell you to keep your child away from boarding school. I am not however a fan of boarding schools that embellish the truth of who and what they are. Some schools are in existence to serve the teachers, trustees and administration, and have little time for the voice of the children. That's a refrain I've heard uttered many times in my travels. You are a parent, and you know how precious your child's voice is, even when she has erred. The lack of desire to hear the voice of the child is the greatest weakness of a boarding school, and exactly the reason that this book exists. No school is worth the amount of money you will pay if they steadfastly refuse to listen to the voice of the child. Not that they must obey the child, but they must listen. As you search for a boarding school, search for the ideal. None will meet that platitude, but many will come close, and in those places your child will be supported, guided, and nourished as he blossoms into a young adult with strength of character, mind, and body. Any less is simply not acceptable.

"...and so the tale is done."

Having completed your journey through Tim Hillman's *Behind the Walls*, you have experienced the insights of a veteran educator and a thoughtful observer of boarding school life across four full and enriching decades. Interestingly, each reader's journey through Tim's book is unique. Prospective parents and students bring with them their individual hopes, aspirations, questions, and concerns; while those who have taught at and/or graduated from boarding schools will find in Tim's analyses reflections of their own memories and experiences.

Full disclosure: I have known Tim Hillman since we were freshmen together at the same Massachusetts boarding school. We lived in the same dorms, attended many of the same classes, earned Varsity letters on some of the same teams, and appeared on stage together in a variety of dramatic productions. At graduation, we actually won the same awards, and we worked for two summers together at a camp for inner-city kids. We both became educators (albeit at different independent boarding schools) and we both write books. He even invited me to write a chapter in one of his earlier works: *Second Home*.

Yet Tim's insights are uniquely his, and he shares with the reader a perception that goes beyond and beneath the standard "rankings" that are ubiquitous in the world of school searches. Parents and students can find specific examples addressing particular concerns. *Behind the Walls* is an illustrated, even virtual, tour of the boarding school experience.

Of course, it is not—it cannot be—all-encompassing. Neither are his observations and conclusions the last word in anything. As he frequently notes, good schools are constantly adapting to an ever-changing world. Good schools continue to address issues like diversity, sexuality, personal responsibility, and parental involvement, and the best schools have met these concerns honestly and sympathetically. At the same time, those very best schools understand that they cannot rest on their laurels, but must continue to adapt and transform, while staying true to the core of their identity and mission. And all schools, good and not-so-good, have individual identities and missions. *Behind the Walls* might just be helpful in finding out what these truly are.

Not every school is for every child, and schools that might not work for one family may be the best thing in the world for another. Tim does not take sides, nor does he ever say that he knows what is best. Rather, he delivers an honest appraisal with eyes wide open. *Behind the Walls* essentially exists to assist parents and students in formulating the right questions to ask when considering a boarding school experience.

You may not agree with everything within these pages. Some anecdotes and examples may have less applicability to some schools than to others. But the only way to find out which school works best for a child's particular needs is to ask the kind of questions that Tim's book encourages and reinforces. A good boarding school experience fosters independence, critical thinking, intellectual curiosity, and both inclusivity and acceptance within a diverse community. Like everything else, including families and other institutions, a boarding school community is a work in progress. Hopefully, reading Behind the Walls has helped you in your efforts to assess that progress. It is not an end in itself, but it can certainly help get you started.

Richard E. "Nick" Noble
    Worcester, Massachusetts

Appendix A

Recommended reading:

Lorene Cary, <u>Black Ice,</u>Vintage, 1992

Louis M. Crosier, Ed., <u>Casualties of Privilege</u>, Gilsum, Avocus
Publishing, 1991

Louis Crosier Ed. <u>Healthy Choices, Healthy Schools</u>, Gilsum, Avocus
Publishing, 1991

Tim Hillman and Craig Thorn, Ed. <u>Second Home: Life in a Boarding
School</u>, Gilsum, Avocus Publishing, 1996

John McPhee <u>The Headmaster,</u> Farrar, Straus and Giroux, 1992

John Knowles <u>A Separate Peace</u>, Scribner, 2003

John Irving <u>A Prayer for Owen Meany</u>, Harper (reprint edition)
2012

Appendix B

Online resources

The Boarding School Review
www.boardingschoolreview.com

Inependent Educational
Consultants Association
www.ieca.org

National Association of Independent Schools
www.nais.org

Secondary Schools Admissions Test
www.ssat.org

Appendix C

Parting Thoughts From an Old Friend (from the first edition)

My friend Tim Hillman has written a book of musings on boarding school life enriched by his usual wit and wisdom. It is a disciplined, thoughtful effort, particularly impressive given the fact that his general manner is the humorist's optimism. I have known Tim for twenty years, and as he has always done, he masters every observation with a Horatian comic's easy intimacy. You will feel, even in Tim's most troubling speculations, a keen desire to confide in the reader every possible way to make the best choice for your child.

Tim does not sensationalize. He does not luxuriate in an insider's penchant for revealed spectacle. Here, Tim has presented a series of brief, direct essays on the essential areas of boarding school life in the spirit of caveat emptor. That he counsels families to be wise even as he promises a successful match if you are careful speaks to the balanced view he offers despite the difficult subjects he addresses.

In Tim's study of boarding schools, you will find his honest appraisal of what can go wrong in a boarding school experience, much of which he demonstrates as the regular vicissitudes of adolescent life exacerbated by the unusual residential setting that finds teenagers in a dormitory on a campus during the school year. However, Tim also shows how boarding schools sometimes build into their structures – residential, academic, financial, cultural, and organizational – behaviors and beliefs that might give you pause.

In other words, while boarding schools in general may argue that they can find a place for just about everybody with decent credentials, boarding schools in particular may fall far short of serving your child's particular needs. What Tim has to say about matters related to coverage (Who is watching your child and when?) is central to residential school and perhaps the most important question a potential boarding school family should bring to the table.

Tim offers useful ways for parents to ask this question and useful ways to judge the answers. At the heart of this book is Tim's genuine concern that parents understand the fundamental trade-off in the boarding school experience. What your child gains from a good boarding school experience – independence, a fine education, a diverse community of peers and adults, facilities, programs, and, yes, prestige – comes at the inevitable cost of residential schooling: when they are there, they are not at home in your house.

With a good boarding school, your child's experience could be worth the trip. With a bad boarding school, your child's experience is a far cry from growing up at home. These possibilities informing Tim's insights and admonitions, the book you have in your hand represents the thoughts and feelings of a good friend who wants to make sure that if you decide to choose boarding school, you make a good choice.

Craig Thorn
Thompson House
Phillips Academy
January 13, 2003

www.ingramcontent.com/pod-product-compliance
Lightning Source LLC
LaVergne TN
LVHW041324080426
835513LV00008B/578